IF YOU LIVE IT
A Pathway to Freedom

There is only one absolute amongst which all is measured: God. May you find yourself always moving towards truth and may you put this book down if you're not ready to know Thyself.

IF YOU LIVE IT

A Pathway to Freedom

By
Mason Burks Wooldridge

Fig Tree Publishing
Another Way Press
49 S Main St STE 411, Pittston, PA 18640
United States of America

Publication
Title: If You Live It, A Pathway to Freedom / by Mason B Wooldridge.
Names: Wooldridge, Mason, author.

Design and layout: Mason B Wooldridge
Cover illustration: Mason B Wooldridge
Edited by: Eddie "The Optimist" Ackerman

Printed in the United States of America by Another Way Press
Distributed by Fig Tree Publishing

ANOTHERWAY
—— PRESS ——

Another Way Press is an imprint of Fig Tree Publishing, and was created and founded by Mason B. Wooldridge, to share truth without edit to concept or practice.

Another Way Press has but one requirement for the books it will accept for the possibility of publishing - they must be truthful, and the truth found within each book must be practiced and lived out by the author, and never just theory or understanding with regards to another's journey of self-discovery.

From Another Way Press and Fig Tree Publishing, thank you for the purchase of this book and for your support. Thank you for the gift of another soul sharing in the truth found within one of our offerings and thank you for being someone whose life is moving towards higher truths, whether you realize that now or not.

Many blessings on your journey into the discovery of Self!

With love,
Mason Burks Wooldridge

WITH THANKS: Without the love and support of a wife who is as beautiful outside as she is inside, and without the kindness of our editor, along with the inspiration from several along the journey who will remain unnamed, including those unaware of their part to play, this book would not have been created and brought to market.

WITH DEDICATION: I dedicate this book to my son, Jeffrey Benjamin Wooldridge. May your light shine brighter than your father's. May your sight stay pointed North. May you find these words your own. And may you be the gift for the world that I already know you to be.

WITH PRAYER: To Thee oh Lord, may this book be your gift to the world. May the pages to follow bring about immense love for the person reading them. May those who find this work be blessed with your proximity. May those who choose a lesser way in this lifetime have this gift waiting for them in the next

CONTENTS

Forward: Page ix
Introduction: Page xii

SECTION ONE: Surrender
    Chapter One: Page 2
    Transcending Shame & Guilt
    Chapter Two: Page 20
    Transcending Apathy & Grief
    Chapter Three: Page 42
    Transcending Fear & Desire

SECTION TWO: Forgiveness
    Chapter Four: Page 60
    Transcending Anger & Pride
    Chapter Five: Page 82
    Experiencing Courage
    Chapter Six: Page 101
    Experiencing Neutrality
    Chapter Seven: Page 114
    Experiencing Willingness
    Chapter Eight: Page 127
    Experiencing Acceptance
    Chapter Nine: Page 141
    Experiencing Reason

SECTION THREE: Gratitude
    Chapter Ten: Page 159
    Experiencing Love
    Chapter Eleven: Page 174
    Witnessing Joy
    Chapter Twelve: Page 190
    Witnessing Peace

Personal Experiences: Page 210
References: Page 219

FORWARD

If coincidences are God's way of reminding us of his presence, then surely irony is His way of amusing himself.

If so, then He must have been delighted a few years ago when the most overwhelming internal fire I'd ever felt came on the coldest day I'd ever experienced.

I questioned my good judgment, and even my sanity, that Saturday morning as I pulled on the double-layered Duofold long underwear my wife had bought for me to wear to a Green Bay Packers playoff game in January of 2012 at Lambeau Field. I wish I could say they kept me warm. They did not, even though the temperature that day in Green Bay climbed to 20 degrees, balmy, by Wisconsin standards.

And here I was, about ten years later, foolishly hoping those Duofolds might provide at least a modicum of comfort on a Pennsylvania morning with a temperature reading of minus 2.

I had made plans to meet a guy for breakfast – a guy I had heard much about but had never before met – and seriously considered calling to cancel. "Besides," I thought, "I bet the place won't even be open. Who'd go out for breakfast on a morning like this?"

It turned out lots of people. To my surprise, the diner was practically full, even some parents with little children, but not nearly as full as would be my heart by the time I left.

Mason Wooldridge has that effect on people.

I had heard Mason's name – interestingly, never his last name – dozens of times during the previous year during my

Sunday morning walks with my friend Joe. Without going into details (they will become clear to anyone reading this book), it was obvious that meeting Mason had changed Joe's life. Joe showed up downright giddy one rainy Sunday when we ran on an elliptical at the gym, and I truly thought he was on something.

I was wrong, but close. He wasn't "on" something. He was "on to" something. The pure freedom and pure love that comes with learning to let go.

Joe kept saying I had to meet Mason, but there was no pressure to set that up. The time would arrive when it was supposed to arrive, Joe said. Which it apparently did. The below zero temp notwithstanding.

Mason told me his story, unvarnished and unembellished, and that's when the fire ignited inside of me. I at first thought it was in my gut, but soon realized it was in my soul.

After breakfast, we stood talking in the diner's parking lot, the cold temperature, which may have climbed to zero by then, be damned. Mason said he had written a book and asked if I would edit it. He said he'd pay me anything I wanted. I told him I'd be honored to be involved but paying me was out of the question.

And that began a two-year process of Mason and me meeting on a regular basis for what we originally had decided would be 90-minute sessions but typically turned into three hours. It began with me reading Mason's book aloud to him and suggesting changes and/or additions, some minor, some adding several pages. When we finished going through the entire manuscript this way, we flipped the script and Mason read the edited book aloud to me, prompting more changes and more additions.

And somewhere in the process, it occurred to me that I had learned what Joe had learned. I learned to let go. Which in essence is learning the power of surrender.

I had always considered myself a follower of Jesus Christ, and still do. I was careful where I stored up my riches, for I knew that is where my heart would be. I strove to put myself last in order to be first, and to lose myself in order to find myself. I loved my neighbor as myself. And now, through Mason, I finally understood how to be in the world and not of the world.

All it took was surrender. Which can only lead to forgiveness. Which can only lead to a life of gratitude. There's a simple word for a life of surrender and forgiveness and gratitude.

That word is love.

If you read this book, embrace its concepts, and do the steps outlined, and if, as the title of this books suggests, you actually live it, you will find yourself living in a world, to borrow Mason's words, where "what some would call miracles happen regularly," and where "joy is a continual reality."

Love, as Mason says, will "fill you up."

But you'll not just experience love. You'll be Love. Take it from me.

- *Eddie Ackerman* (Editor)

INTRODUCTION

Who am I?
What is this book all about?
Why am I sharing this message?
How did this book come to be?
What is the personal ego?
What is fear?
How are the ego and fear related?
How does my level of consciousness affect my surroundings?
How does ego/fear stop me from getting what I desire most?
What are the levels of consciousness and how do they correspond with my happiness/freedom?
Why should I care about raising my level of consciousness and transcending ego/fear?
How can this book help me live the life I have always dreamed of?

...Who am I?

This is an excellent question because it provides context for the rest of the journey we're about to take. What the world today calls Mason has not always been what's present, but what is present now was always a possibility for what the world would get to experience.

I speak of myself in the third person not for the purpose of separation, but for the purpose of description. I was once lost, scared, fearful of the future and worried about the past catching up with me. I was running away from an inevitability I couldn't articulate at a younger age. But I was always out ahead of a calling that seemed never to be within my grasp.

Today, I am the byproduct of a fully surrendered life, a life the world would see as a linear movement through time like most with a job and a family, dogs and a house, but these are not the things that define what or who I am. I have experienced highs and lows, and not unlike you reading this today, I *survived* most of my life, as opposed to *getting out of the way* of Life. Which was necessary in order that this life could take on a meaning and significance far greater than what I thought possible as a youth growing up in a perpetual state of confusion.

As a child, I grew up for a time with a mother and father married and building a life together. At an early age, my parents decided to go their separate ways, with custody of me going to my mom and the "fun" weekends being spread out occasionally with my dad. For the most part, my mother raised me with the help of a stepfather and the loving kindness of grandparents from my father's side. I had aunts and uncles on both sides, cousins and brothers, but by growing up in a divorced household early on, what I didn't know until much later in adulthood was life for me moving into the future would never be stable again like it was within the first few years of coming into a body as an infant.

Shortly after my 11th birthday, my father passed away and life took on a new meaning: wondering why he died, where he went, what happens once we all die, and wondering what the point of being alive was. All of a sudden, as if out of nowhere, after the death of my dad, I had more questions about life than I had answers. I was left to wander the earth without a father to show me the way. My mom, who did her best to love me and provide support, did a great job living for me until she had other obligations with regards to a new husband and new children. Looking back, Mom made decisions believing remarriage would mean a better life for us than she thought possible on her own, but as a young child, I hated her for remarrying and having new kids to give her time and attention to.

As the years progressed from childhood into adolescence, and from adolescence into young adulthood, I lived mostly at Fork Union Military Academy – "Where boys go to become men" – in central Virginia. It was a boarding school for most boys there, but I was one of the handful of what they called "day students," which meant I spent the day there but went home at night to sleep in a bed not provided by the school. At this school, I met boys from around the world and had teachers who appeared to be fully formed men. I made lifelong friendships with a few such people and generally look back on the years I spent within the walls of that school as fond times and happy memories, but only in hindsight, after I became an adult. You quickly forget the "shared misery" that was our everyday life as 12-year-old "cadets."

Fork Union Military Academy was founded and instituted within the Southern Baptist Church, which meant chapel service was a regular thing more than twice a week, with religion playing a central role in the discipleship of young men and the lives they would lead there and out into the world thereafter. As a student, I loved the days we had chapel and the lessons the bible taught throughout the course of several different chaplains during my time in uniform. I was searching for answers to life's biggest questions, and between the discipline of military school, guidance of mature men, and the word of God being pumped into my veins daily through our motto "Body, Mind and Spirit," I felt more whole than broken.

Most days. I would arrive home at the end of the day, however, and be reminded that my dad was dead. And my mom had a new family. And the way my brain worked then, home life seemed to be where the questions about heaven and hell and life and death resumed their plague on me.

As I matured and aged into teen years, as well as into young adult years, I had questions that started off as wonderings that never got fully answered. And they became full-blown issues with the faith of Christianity and the inability to have men of the cloth provide real answers about faith and God that felt authentic and genuine. I found myself growing up with more questions than answers yet again, despite the guidance of more quality men in my life than many could ever hope for.

My mother and stepfather were not rich people. Actually, far from it. I grew up for most of my young life on a farm owned by my step grandparents, and I would classify our financial situation as one of living paycheck to paycheck most months. I was able to attend a pricey military school because when my father passed away the federal government saw to it I received his Social Security benefits until I turned 18 or graduated from high school, whichever came last.

I was always older than my classmates after being held back in kindergarten for being emotionally too juvenile to pass into first grade. It was like a scene in a movie. I told my teacher I had to use the bathroom and when she wouldn't let me, I peed my pants. I thought about writing "tinkle," but it was more than a tinkle. A lot more. It was on purpose, too. It was out of defiance, a deliberate action, the outward expression of the emotional trauma of a 5-year-old kid. But it was enough to dictate that I would not graduate from Grasshopper Green with the rest of my class.

As I look back on childhood, I had what felt like a normal upbringing, but in all reality, it wasn't. However, as I've aged, I know my story is far from as rough as many kids across the world have it. But nonetheless, it was formative and full of lessons learned. I was never without food to eat or clothes to wear, even though I would have liked other types of food and different clothes. I was never without a male role model worth listening to despite my stubbornness at times to listen or pay attention to their wisdom. I was never without love and friendships, but I didn't always notice them in times of deep sorrow and depression, rage, anguish, and moments of wanting to die. Yes, wanting to die. As far back as 11 years old, to follow my dad.

Teenage angst often results in thoughts of ending one's life, but somewhere in that 11th year I knew there was nothing more important to me than "Is there a God?" And if there wasn't, then what was the point of me staying here any longer? At 11, every big question that everyone has in their life presented itself to me in a cascading fashion. Divinity finally presented itself at 20, but for nine straight years I asked those questions every day, 365 days a year. "Trauma Informed Care" was not a thing back then, but looking back, I sure was a perfect candidate for it. Some thought I didn't care about school. I did, but what I cared about more, what was central to everything I cared about, was "Is God real?"

I had a way with girls and enjoyed having a girlfriend, and if you had asked my coaches at the time, I enjoyed having a girlfriend a little too much. As I look back on childhood, I can say with confidence, I was made to be a searcher of truth from an early age. I was filled with discontent and a longing to be free to find out what the world was made of and what my place was within it. I had dreams of waking up as an adult and being free of what felt like an oppressive life, and not unlike many reading this, I was actually spoiled by God with how good life was compared to many others in the world.

Without having a biological father around, I looked for others to be my dad, and almost every time I found a man who loved me and was older, I latched on to him and grew attached. As if marching to a drum beat, every man I grew attached to was there for a season but not a lifetime, save a couple. But at the time I wasn't concerned with forever. I was concerned with the here and now and receiving the abundance of attention I felt I deserved for just being alive.

I spent many weekends with my grandparents in Lynchburg, Virginia, about an hour or so from Fork Union, and with those trips came more family I could grab onto for love and support. Some of my fondest memories of growing up were surrounded by the family I escaped to on weekends, and later the family I escaped to during the week who were not my biological own. I was constantly moving as a young person, always wondering about life, always praying to God, always questioning what the world told me, and always looking for something that would complete me, or at least provide enough peace of mind to let me rest a weary head for a while and not notice life was continuing to move along without my help.

I found sports as an outlet, not unlike many kids around the world. And I dedicated myself to being a sport's star with aspirations to play Division 1 basketball. Something happens when you don't have a dad. You're either a dastardly kid who doesn't care about anything, or you worry about everything. I don't have to tell you which one I was (the kindergarten peeing incident notwithstanding), but there was no end to my worrying.

Even in fifth grade I recall walking along Route 15 near our home in Buckingham County and saying to my mom, "There's no need to save for college because I'm going to get a basketball scholarship." And that kind of cemented my persona at the time.

The funny thing is, if I remember correctly, I wasn't even any good at basketball. I was sort of tall for my age but I didn't hit a growth spurt until junior high school. I went from 5'6 to 6'1 over my seventh-grade year and was 6'3 by the time I was a freshman. I continued to grow until I leveled off at 6'6 well into my 20s. It seemed like overnight I went from not hitting my head on doorways to hitting my head on doorways. In many ways that conversation with my mom set in motion the opportunity to achieve that goal of a scholarship. She explained to me that I was receiving Social Security benefits because of my dad's death and we could either start putting it away for college, or I could use it right now to attend a private school where I might be able to enhance my basketball talents, such as they were. That school was Fork Union.

I hated where I lived in Buckingham County and the only way out I saw was as a basketball player. It was not that I loved basketball, it was that basketball, as I saw it, was my ticket. I worked my entire life to get a scholarship, and even though I wasn't the best athlete or the strongest physical specimen, I managed after years of toil and countless hours spent past high school still pursuing this dream, to land a scholarship to one of America's greatest colleges.

Here's how it went. Starting in sixth grade I was a student at Fork Union, wearing a military uniform, shaving before I had peach fuzz, spit shining my shoes (with actual spit) and taking showers with other young men who actually had body hair. There's a world of difference between a sixth grader and an eighth grader. I would wind up setting a record for longest tenure at Fork Union Military Academy stretching over nine years. I would graduate in 2003 and not leave until 2005.

And here's how that went. Despite my promise to my mom and my lofty expectations and pronouncements, in sixth grade I didn't even go out for basketball. I went out for swimming. But I wound up going one day to swim practice and never going back. The warm up was something like 25 or 50 laps before we even started practice. I was holding onto the side of the pool wondering "What am I doing?" I showed up at the second day of basketball try-outs instead of the first and still made the team.

Looking back, there were so many men who had my best interests at heart. Steve Macek, the junior high coach and our science teacher, had every right to tell me go play intramurals because I missed that first day. But I think he knew I was a broken kid and maybe needed a "quicker" second chance that others.

I played through my senior year at Fork Union and while I made All Conference, helped the team to our first post-season playoff berth in several years, and was named captain, my dream of a Division I scholarship seemed unrealistic. I had a number of Division II and Division III offers, but it wasn't until the summer after graduation that the University of Buffalo, a Division I program, called with an offer. But by then I had committed to returning to Fork Union as a post graduate.

During the summer of my junior and senior years I attended Five Star Basketball Camp, in Farmville, Virginia, at Hampton Sydney College. Both summers I made the all-star team. One year, Chris Paul was the point guard on the team I played on. As an aside, Stephen Colbert attended Hampton Sydney.

My freshman year I had a very important coach in Coach Rogers – Coach "Roge" to us. He had played at Virginia Tech. At 6'9 he was scary and intimidating. He was a no B-S guy. That's the year I actually dared to believe I could play Division I because I made the team as a freshman for that coach with that team. He was such a good coach that the last game of our season, we played Blue Ridge, a basketball power, which turned out to be a game that exemplified our poor attitude and as a result Coach refused to take us to the playoffs. That was a powerful life lesson he deemed more important than a chance at winning a state basketball championship.

Fork Union was a basketball and football factory. Heisman Trophy winners Vinny Testaverde and Eddie George played football at Fork Union. At one time, there were 27 Fork Union grads actively playing in the NFL. Kevin Plank, founder of Under Armour, was a post-grad football player at Fork Union and, thanks to him, everywhere you look at Fork Union, from uniforms to underwear, you'll see the UA logo. The post-grad program was legendary, in both sports. In basketball, during any given year there were at least one and perhaps three high level college coaches, from such programs as Duke, Kentucky, North Carolina, sending preferred recruits to Fork Union for seasoning. There would be 12 players on the team. Those not sent from high level collegiate programs, were potential mid-major talents, and the rest all had similar potential.

We had Wednesday night and Saturday night "open gym" for our first month on campus, say August 25 through October 1, and 10 to 20 coaches from around the country would be on hand on Wednesday night and 20 to 30 top college coaches on Saturday. When I was allowed to practice with the team during my under-grad years I saw every big-name coach in the stands: Rick Pitino, Dean Smith, Bill Self, you name it.

The reason I was there with these older guys, all top college recruits, was because during the summer of my freshman going into sophomore year, Coach Fletcher Arritt, arguably the greatest prep basketball coach of all time, came looking for me. Coach Arritt was the reason for Fork Union's post graduate program success.

He was an example of integrity before I knew what that was. Two things were important about that summer conversation. One was he told me I should pick one sport and focus on it. Baseball had been my first sport since my time in Little League. Coach Arritt told me I had more potential to play college basketball than baseball. "You need to pick one or the other," he said, "and should you pick basketball. I want to extend an invitation to you to practice with us before and after your season starts." By "us" he meant that legendary post-grad team. Accepting that invitation would put me in a position, as a 6'3, 165 pound nobody, next to, say, a potential All-American sent there from Kentucky.

More importantly than basketball, what that conversation set in motion was Coach Arritt's beliefs becoming my beliefs. My sophomore and junior seasons were unremarkable. Coach Roge had left for a local public school after my first year, and during the next two years, I played an equal amount for our new coach as I did as a freshman playing with future Heisman Trophy finalist, Chris Perry, who wound up a future running back for Michigan. The point is, I had no growth as a player.

By the end of my junior season my mother and I started

looking for another school to attend because of the lack of opportunity at Fork Union due to the coaching change and a completely different style of play. But right before the end of my junior year, Brooks Berry, who had married Coach Arritt's daughter, moved back to Fork Union and took over as the varsity basketball coach. And, enthused and rejuvenated, I decided to stay for my senior year.

My senior year was a complete reversal from the previous two years. I went from hardly playing to starting, being leading scorer, making All Conference. One of the reasons senior year produced a different result was because Coach Brooks ran everything that Coach Arritt ran, which was everything I practiced every summer: Passing game, Carolina transition, man to man defense. Funny, I only remember one single play from that senior year. We played Woodbury Forrest in the Prep League. I had never beaten WF in the three previous years of high school. The last game of the regular season, we were up maybe 10 or 12 points with 30 seconds left. A teammate got a steal and I tomahawked a dunk. I felt amazing and I started celebrating. The whistle blows. Coach Brooks pulls me out of the game. As he sat me on the bench, he instilled a very valuable lesson. Which is you can win without setting yourself up for future failure. "We may have to face them in the playoffs," he said. "We don't want to give them more motivation."

Coach Brooks was a fierce competitor. He started for West Virginia University and was an All-Conference player in the Big East as a 6'6 white guy. He was unique. He once kicked a basketball in anger at practice and then immediately apologized. He was the first "older brother" I had that I chose that was not biologically related to me. It created high expectations for both sides. He saw a lot of me in him, especially regarding potential. He set a goal for me for the season: 4 to 6 points and 3 rebounds a quarter. I came pretty close to achieving it.

There were 127 kids in my graduating class. Everyone was leaving for greener pastures. They all knew where they were going and it was listed in the handout at graduation. One says Harvard. Another the Naval Academy. Another Virginia Tech. Mine says Fork Union. Yep, the very school I was graduating from. I was coming back to the military academy for a post-graduate year.

I remember being grateful Coach Arritt was giving me a spot on his team. There was hesitancy because I'd have to go from being a day student to living there as a cadet. As a post grad, you attend classes just like a high school student. But the structure was a one-subject plan. One subject all day for seven weeks. Five classes in a year. The one subject plan was perfect for improving SAT scores, or taking a class you failed. I took two sessions of SAT prep with Col. Dennis Brown where all we did was prep. My scores went up 300 points just knowing how to take the test. Col. Brown was one of the most brilliant and loving teachers I've ever known. He'd take the practice SAT in English along with us and get a perfect score. But not tell anyone.

First post grad year, 2003-2004, I woke up with a sore throat. First practice, something was physically way off. My closed throat was diagnosed as mononucleosis and a throat infection. It hospitalized me in our campus infirmary for five weeks where I basically withered away. I was 185 to 190 pounds going in. When I finally got out of bed, I was 152. I took three Percocet every three and half hours to be even able to swallow applesauce.

And that was the first time I ever planned how to kill myself.

Both times in my life when I realistically thought of ending my life, I thought: if I don't die what am I going to do then?

I don't know if it's a lucky or an unlucky thing to have your persona shattered. But when I stood in front of the mirror and saw my body withering away, the only thing I had wanted in life, to escape Buckingham County, was disappearing before my eyes. I was becoming a skeleton. Going from the potential of being a recruited Division I basketball player to being barely able to make it from the hospital bed to the bathroom.

I was shattered.

In the south you have these pine trees everywhere. On the first floor, where my room was, I looked out at these pine trees. On the other side were the blacktopped basketball courts. Could I jump through the glass and let the shattered window panes cut me and let me bleed out?

I had to reconcile this lost dream and I didn't see any hope. I had just turned 19. It must have been a month and a half later my throat issues had calmed down. I was able to go back and practice again. At the start of the season we always scrimmaged Oak Hill, one of the top high school basketball programs nationally. Carmelo Anthony went there. It was loaded with fifth year seniors and regular seniors. It was truly a basketball factory, sponsored by the Jordan brand. It was the North Carolina or Duke of high school basketball. Coach Arritt wanted to see us against the best. I was able to practice enough to get in the game against point guard Rajon Rondo and forward Josh Smith. Rondo wound up with an NBA Championship with both the Boston Celtics and Los Angeles Lakers and Smith went on to win the slam dunk contest when he played with the Atlanta Hawks. Smith was drafted out of high school six months after I played against him. Playing against them was humiliating but also created a fire to not give up. I may have gotten in 5 to 7 minutes. I was so emaciated, I was nowhere ready to compete. Trying to guard Rondo, I came off the help side to greet him at the rim. He just he-maned me with his right hand, creating six feet of space and had an easy left-hand layup. He was 6'4 with a 7-foot wingspan. I was immediately substituted for. I was embarrassed at the degree of which he was a better player but a fire was lit to let this not be the last chapter in my basketball journey. Once we got back to campus, Coach Arritt came to me and said I needed to take the whole year off. And that academic year came to an end.

I spent the rest of the year rehabbing at home, getting a job, not knowing when I left if I'd have a spot next year on the team. But pretty soon after being home, Coach Arritt called and said why don't you come back again? A couple of things had happened. When my tonsils were taken out, I was able to put on weight and muscle. I came back for my second post grad year a man.

There had been only one team that recruited me during my sickness year, and that was the Air Force Academy. Both of my PG years, 03-05, Air Force had been a top 25 team and made the NCAA tournament two years in a row. The AF Academy was a legit basketball presence. The one school I had wanted to go to was University of Pennsylvania. Coach Arritt took me up there. He was friends with Coach Dunphy.

Something I didn't know was how good I would be when I came back for the second PG year. Real good. Coach Arritt had shielded me from a lot of stuff. He was grooming me for life, a blessed life. He knew I had the grades and skills to get into many schools, even Ivy League, but he knew I was a broken kid who could get lost in the wrong program. He knew what schools would be best for me, and never even told me there had been ACC interest. As a team we finished 28 and 2, number 2 or 3 in the country, losing our last game of the season with a shot at sharing the number one spot in the country to finish out the year. I had pulled a groin muscle, which meant while I became a ranked player nationally during the first half of the season, I played limited minutes over the second half. During the season, while injured, I committed to the Air Force Academy. They had continued to recruit me. I looked on it as an opportunity to play high major Division I basketball, with a Princeton style offense which I knew I fit into. Also, Air Force was going to pay for law school.

The reality of coming back for the PG years had more to do with pleasing Coach Arritt and honoring his belief in me than it had to do with wanting to play Division I basketball. Deep down, somewhere in the darkest recesses of my being, I knew I didn't like basketball or having to play it. My body knew this reality as well and would do its best to show me the error of my choices through the gastrointestinal system and regular issues I had with it throughout my time competing at high levels of the sport. Your stomach is a natural truth teller. Most people have an inner psychic and for most it's located right below the chest.

I stopped having fun with the sport once I realized it was hard work to be good at it. I stopped wanting to play the sport when I stopped getting praise for just dribbling a basketball. Nevertheless, I accepted a scholarship to college at the D1 level with the hopes to put aside all of the doubt about wanting to continue playing.

Almost immediately after the death of my father, the only thing ever on my mind, except for brief respites with girls, was an agony in searching for truth. Almost every waking hour was spent either praying to God about why I was here and the point of everything or spent mad at God for the life I was currently living. All in all, at the time, I didn't like being a kid, nor a teenager. I always felt like life was going to take place away from teenage years and not amongst the life of someone just able to drive and still attending biology class. Although my story may be better or worse than others reading this with regards to life's circumstances, and I'm not covering the full gambit here in this writing as to the traumas totally discovered. What I now know about growing up that was different from almost every other child on this planet, was the constant dialogue I had with God about life, the constant need for answers to the holes found within the Bible and its corresponding religion, and the reasons for death and life that were constantly present within daily mental discourse which always came up short of making sense.

Once making it to the age of 18, I started shifting in my approach to God, and I stopped praying to the Creator out of anger and spite. I instead started a journey of interest in the occult and praying directly to my father to make a connection. I grew interested in spirits, angels, demons and the afterlife, but from the vantage point of curiosity and not deliverance. I had moments of genuine experience with a world outside of my daily life during these pursuits, and enough spooky moments over time to limit my desire to continue being exposed to what is usually left unseen. Always close to my mind was God, and I was always working an angle to know more about truth and life, about why I was here on this planet, and what the point of this life was all about. There was constantly something within my being that knew I was here for something other than what I could put into words or dared allowed to become a reality. It wasn't that I knew I was destined for great things as much as I had hopes I would do something to change the world for the better. I looked for love in any place I thought could provide it, but always came back thirsty for another source and outlet for greater love and further intensity of spirit.

I started dabbling in drugs and alcohol after graduating high school but before leaving for college. I was having sex with anyone I could find, and I was starting to not necessarily drift away from God, but more be ashamed to approach God, all the while wanting more and more answers to questions that had been present for many years up until this point.

Just before I left for college, I paid one last visit to my grandparents to say goodbye, and while there I decided to also say goodbye to a close friend of theirs who lived across the street who had also been a part of my life since I could remember. Granny Doris, as I called her. It was purely out of affection and I could tell she appreciated it. She was the only person I knew who felt truly godly to me other than my grandmother. But Granny Doris had a different aura to her, something magical and even close to God. She was spooky. In a good way. She was someone I respected and loved, but someone I kept some distance from because of her obvious proximity to divinity. What I know now is she was unconditional love personified. And when someone is unconditional love as a level of consciousness, they are used within the world in a different way than most on the earth. They're saints. They're life-changers. They're connected. And they have a connection which is them and not because of them.

As I made my way over to see her, not more than a week before leaving town for good and possibly never coming back, I had no idea what was to come next, nor how it would change the course of my life forever. I always went to her back door. On this day with each step, the title of the book "The Unbearable Lightness of Being" is an apt way to describe how I felt. Except, it was more akin to a bearable lightness of being. It was a beckoning. A pulling sensation. A knowingness of "I have to go here." If you've had that feeling of, "I don't know why I'm going here, but I have to go here," you have some idea of what was taking place.

I could have classified the previous ten years since losing my father as an unbearable burden of being. I can feel even to this day, the sensation of taking those steps and almost everything about that night. I moved past my grandparents' house and down the sidewalk adjacent to the main road they lived on. I crossed the road and started down the sidewalk in front of her house. I walked up her driveway towards the house gleeful and full of what felt to be increasing joy, and then moved my hand to knock on her door. As my hand went to knock, the door opened and there she was, my other granny, standing in the dimly lit room she used as a sun porch, but which at night held little light, save whatever sidelamp she had on.

As long as I knew her, we used the sunporch for conversations. Only one other time in my life had I seen other parts of her home, and it was the night I stayed with her before my father's funeral. However, on this night, she ushered me in with a smile and moved me right along to another part of her house known as the formal living room. For those of you who are not familiar with the customs of the South, every traditional family incorporates a "formal living room." No TV. Usually a fire place. Obviously opulent. Where shoes were never worn. Whose chairs were rarely sat on. And which was rarely used.

I knew as we walked back into her home that something was already different about this evening. And it wasn't just because the door opened as I began to knock, or because I felt lighter in spirit just walking over to see her, or because we were entering a part of her home I had never spent time in before. It was because her manner and complexion were different from any other time I had seen her. Her face was angelic, her aura was radiant, and the moment we sat down together – she in a single high-back chair and I, separated by a coffee table, seated on a wooden-armed double-seated couch, which someone who bought their furniture in the '70s would have called a love seat and asked specifically for the wooden arms – a smile arose not only over my face but over my entire being.

As we smiled at one another, the mood of the room grew intimate and the light grew ominous in a good way. I can't remember exactly the words used to start the conversation but what came next was apparently the reason I felt convicted earlier to go see her. Once pleasantries were exchanged and niceties conveyed, the conversation took on a different caliber of importance and the light in the room grew dense with love and a growing radiance of perfected presence. The room was literally changing before my very eyes, and not in a way where one grows accustomed to changing light from leaving a darker area, but in a way where the room was starting to glow with what felt like omniscience, omnipresence and omnipotence.

Somewhere in the sensation of the evening, as the light changed and the mood lightened towards being surrounded by a presence of God I had never before felt, the movement of my lips and hers stopped taking place, and our conversation became one of the energies of our souls communicating without the use of either mouth or voice box. As a question would arise from within my being, it would be answered from within hers. As questions would cease from my angle, from her beingness came the request for further questions to be asked, which created the next question to present itself. I remember distinctly noticing throughout our time together that her lips weren't moving, but her gaze was fixed upon mine and a smile was permanently gracing the face of a heavenly presence.

The room continued to transcend the energy most people commonly feel when going about life, and the light grew more abundant and all encompassing. I felt relaxed and almost coddled in the grace of the room and the presence of what I could not deny was some aspect of divinity. God, the infinite creator, was present in a way not known until that point. But the fullness of God was not present, nor can it be while still attached to this body. But some aspect of God was more than abundant and filling me up simultaneously with honesty, love, and an openness to ask any question that came into awareness.

I asked about life and death, my father, the meaning of life and existence, and eventually about why I was here on this planet and what my purpose for this life was. Intermixed between questions and answers were directive statements towards my being of what I was doing to create distance between myself and the creator, and what the future was to hold in the weeks and months and years to immediately follow the conversation.

I was told about my purpose for being alive, and never during the time spent with God that night through the presence of someone whose life was dedicated to God, was there ever a moment of disbelief about what was transpiring, or what the moment at hand represented against previously held beliefs about the reality of God being real or fake. There was no attachment to time or space, and until the time with God in this way came to an end, there was no exchange with time as it was before walking into this room. As the final question was answered and the last statement of internal prophecy was summoned forth, the room grew quiet again as the light that once filled the place in an unimaginable way subsided into the regular glow of proper side lamps.

As the room became just based on the awareness of two people seated facing one another, the conversation came to a sweet but final end. As we walked to the back door for me to exit, Granny Doris was back to who she was, a sweet and love-filled, godly woman who wore a youthful smile on her face with glad tidings to see me off.

I left her home that night and walked slowly back towards my biological grandparents' home. I knew life would never be the same for me again. How could it? God just talked to me, and all the questions I ever had were answered. I continued to make my way across the street and onto my family's property, and as I walked through their front door, I was left speechless about what had transpired.

As the night continued to move along, I have little recollection about how the evening ended and what conversations I had with my Granny and Pop about what happened, except I know I didn't tell them, and I never told them about the angel who lived across the street, nor about the conversation with some aspect of divinity that would wind up changing the course of my life from that night forward.

The next day I awoke and felt changed but also had a

lingering question born into awareness that would mark the beginning of the next 12 years of my life: how do I do what I'm here to do, and be who I'm here to be, if I don't have any answers worth giving to people?

One thing that was shared with me that night was the reality that the school I was leaving for was not my final destination, and that I wouldn't be there long. This turned out to be excruciatingly true, and within the next two months I had not only left for college but returned from it as well.

Over the course of the next decade-plus of life, I chased after answers to new questions, questions born out of an internal knowingness about my path for this life long-term. I felt haunted by knowing the future as time went on because I never felt ready or capable of being what I was here to be.

I felt lost because the answers to the questions I had were not found within the religion I grew up with, nor were they to be found by living a life of quiet desperation. I was a man with a flag but no hill to plant it on. I wandered aimlessly out in the wilderness for many years, searching high and low for truth and often times winding up face down in a puddle of my own vomit and tears. My searching was always there but the fear of never reaching the life purpose this time around became like a heavy noose carried around the neck, and over time, instead of righteously surveying the world for answers to questions, I chose to hide from even looking for the answers for fear I'd never find them.

I started a career as a professional womanizer and drinker. I started other careers as a pothead and a liar. I spent days and weeks trying to wrestle with the reality that I knew my purpose, but would never live up to it. I was scared, fearful of the present, the future, the past, and everything in-between.

I made deals with God along the way about doing something else instead with career choices, and each time I tried to hide within the confines of a decent life, one the world would hold as worthy. I would self-destruct or lose that opportunity because it wasn't the final place for me the whole time, only unrecognized stepping stones. God continued to do for me what I was unable to do for myself, which was keep me moving towards a determined end where choice would be made simple, and in the meantime experience all that the world had to offer so that the answer to the final question would be one of knowingness and not one of wondering further.

Finally, years later, I found myself on the fateful night of choice in a living hell, separated from love, from God, from humanity, and in a place where an eternity separated from hope felt real and overwhelming. I had chased the answers to the questions about God far and wide out in the world and come up empty, depressed, beaten down and close to death. My study of this world had come to an end, and either I was going to graduate back into grace and acceptance, or I was going to die and miss the chance at redemption. I had reached a final jump-off point where I was now a full member of the world, alcoholic and all, and either the world was going to be the end of the road or God was going to be the choice made after hiding for 12 years.

On July 4th, 2017, time stopped somewhere in the early evening hours and God showed up in a way that was undeniable yet again. After years on the lamb with regards to living out a higher purpose for being in the body, I came face-to-face with a choice, a choice which presented itself other times before, but this time when the choice was presented there was a knowingness it would be the last of its kind: choose Life and another way or choose death and have to do it all over again. Subjectively, time stopped, and the world phased out of focus, the body stopped feeling and the mind was no longer obeying any thought patterns related to previous moments leading up until right then. As vision was reduced to a single internal knowingness without any doubt presenting itself, an inaudible voice came from within screaming softly that the moment at hand is vastly different from the moments catalogued prior. What the moment and knowingness presented was simple, but what was a person to do with the ultimatum built on a current foundation of denying a better way to live so far?

To set the context for the immenseness of this choice, it is vital to know that after 12 years of running from God, I was now a raging alcoholic. Anyone who has gone through a 12-step program is familiar with this definition of insanity: doing the same thing over and over and expecting a different result. Anyone who has battled addiction of any sort in their lives fully knows the veracity of this definition. For me, God's grace that night lifted the veil of insanity and allowed me to see what my life had truly become. At this point drinking wasn't fun anymore. In truth it hadn't been for some time. Those days were long gone if they had ever truly been there at all. It had gotten to the point where drinking became medicine to hide from the constant fears the mind managed to manifest once drinking no longer became just a casual past-time. I was drinking because I feared success, but not success in the way most people would think about it. I feared the type of success that meant I knew what my purpose in life was and part of the reason I was alive, but I couldn't imagine ever living up to it, or for more clarity, I had no clue how to get from point "A" where the truth was known, to point "B," where the truth manifested as reality.

Twelve years almost to the day after seeing God for the first time through Granny Doris, I had come full circle to a time paused once again by the presence of God posing this question of life or death. Despite the many times I chose differently in the past, this time with an equally reckless abandon, I was ready to give life one last shot and accept God's outstretched arm. That night, I chose Life over the world, Life over insanity, Life over death and what vanished immediately was a desire to take another drink or make any further decisions rooted in fear. And just like that, based on a single, divinely inspired choice, I was transported back in time to a reality where life in front of me was worth more than what got left behind.

Almost instantly, once saying yes to a higher truth and good-bye to a life of hiding, the same connection to a wordless divinity felt all those years prior re-presented itself as if no time passed at all, as if forgiveness isn't attached to time but outside of it just waiting on its string to be pulled. The gift of instant forgiveness erased all of the time running, and all that was left was the sense in the immediate timeframe that not only had God not gone anywhere nor forgotten about me, but grace was always there with an outstretched hand just waiting for me to accept the handshake.

On July 4th, 2017, God pulled me from the depths of a living hell to the heights of a subjective reality where love was more present than at any other time in memory. That night, for the first time in many years, the clouds above my head parted ways and allowed sunshine to sparkle unabated, and for the first time in a long while, all the fears that filled the mind and body earlier in the previous hours, days, weeks, months and years were gone. Ultimately replaced with the subjective experience of warmth on the soul and daylight on the face of life yet to be lived.

Unlike other times in the past when I pleaded for God's help with the outcomes of poor decision making, and then after experiencing some relief as a result went right back to making the same poor decisions, this time I put resolve and promise into action steps when presented with Life as an actionable choice. I found myself immediately moving towards help in the form of a 12-step program. Along with the 12-step group, I found the written works of a couple people important for the next phase of life's journey: Byron Katie and Dr. David R. Hawkins.

Byron Katie was the first author I found in the self-help world that allowed me to put her work to practice, and the outcome of doing so was a major revelation: we have thoughts but we're not our thoughts. Quickly, what followed was the realization that we have a mind but we're not the mind, and if these two revelations were correct, logically what followed is that we have a body but we're not the body. And in cascading fashion, many other similar revelations sprang forth into consciousness leaving me as the host effortlessly moving towards higher and higher truths.

Dr. Hawkins became my greatest spiritual teacher next to what would come later in the recognition and appreciation for Jesus and Krishna. Dr. Hawkins had done something no other person had throughout history, he created a quantifiable chart of understanding consciousness (the characteristic of God which we call omniscience), and with the help of his teachings and the use of his chart, I began charting my own progress from hell to heaven and applying what was learned into my own knowingness of the world around me and how it works.

As the magic of working the 12-steps began manifesting

within my physical and mental life, spiritually I was experiencing something growing more and more powerful within every daily experience. Love was filling me up. From July 4th, 2017, until the moment of writing this, life has morphed from danger to physical life to the regular experience and witness of God as imminent. What I feared impossible at age 20, fully manifested as reality on March 21st, 2018, when the full realization of God as Self set in for the first time. Life was never about physicality again, nor was it about fear in any form or love limited in any way. The peace of inner ecstasy that was ushered into being was unmistakable, and the way in which I now operated within the world made it clear subjectively that the reality of God was self-evident and self-revealing, omniscient, omnipotent and omnipresent. At this point, it is not pertinent to elaborate on the states of consciousness you'll find escalating within this book, or the states of enlightenment that became a reality over 2018 and beyond, but suffice to say, subjectively, life today is nothing like life before March 21st, 2018, just like life on July 3rd, 2017, was nothing like life on July 4th, 2017.

Consciousness went from experiencing hell as an experiential reality, to experiencing life in such a way no limits remained, and where heaven is a known reality while on this plane of existence as well as a reality when one leaves the physical body behind. Consciousness didn't stop evolving in an upwards trajectory after the initial onslaught of higher truth settled in as a new subjective reality, but from the undeniable physical and spiritual sensations of all-encompassing ecstasy that goes along with Satcitananda, or the realization of God as Self.

Now, every moment of every day is without definition or attachment, perfect in nature, without wants, desires, cravings, fears, or poor decision-making fueling the next highest choice. Today, like sages who have reported similar states of old, I can attest to the fact that at a certain level of consciousness, the reality of divinity becomes known and not just read about, and what some would call miracles, happen regularly now as the unfoldment of every moment presenting itself anew.

Today, synchronicity and miracles are commonplace, and today, I can honestly say to all of you reading this, one has to do nothing, save regular surrender, forgive everyone for everything and witness the gratitude arising which follows, in order to have a life only dreamed about.

What was made known over time was the gift at the center of the 12-step program, and through both of Katie's and Hawkins's work, was the power of surrender, and by which the mind/ego can be transcended, leaving only truth as observable, and along with it a constant and genuine happiness mixed with perfected contentment. Today, joy is present as a continual reality, and it's not conditioned upon someone else's response to me or how the world treats this personage, it's an internal joy present in knowingness which transcends understanding. Today, there is no longer a person present separate from anyone else or the world around me, what is present is an awareness that enlightenment is the byproduct of setting one's intent north and chasing after God through the continual surrendering over of the lesser for the greater. A person doesn't become enlightened, just like a person isn't their body. Enlightenment sets in like a condition. But unlike a physical condition, enlightenment is experienced as the lens through which reality is witnessed and observed. No person is enlightened, but once enlightenment sets in, what someone in this state of consciousness knows is there is no individual person present, now or anytime in the past. Just as known is that God is not somewhere else in the universe, but everywhere in the universe at the same time, as well as being that which writes these words now. And no different from that which reads these words now.

God is imminent as well as transcendent, everywhere, all things, all the time. God is here and there, not just over there observing over here. God is not singular and in a single place awaiting a single time. God is plural and all the time, just in varying degrees of truth present within subjective realities. What we all are, as much as can be described through words, can be understood in what follows here: *I, in greater or lesser degree of intensity.*

Today, I, like you, are a degree of consciousness being expressed in greater or lesser quantities of love and truth present. I am also what you see me as, but just like God, we're much more than what we usually see when we look out into the world. I am a byproduct of a surrendered life and of God doing for me what I could not do for myself: delivering me from lost to found, hurt to free, pained to healed, and now a mirror for the world to see God smiling back at them. I am an example for everyone reading this book that you are never too far gone, too far out of reach, too far left or right of center, never outside of God's love. If I can have a witness of God today the way it manifests itself, so can you. No matter the hell you may find yourself in. No matter the miles you have traveled for answers to some of life's biggest questions. Truth and grace are just a choice away.

...What is this book all about?

This book is a byproduct of the altered states experienced, witnessed and observed today by the author, as well as what was experienced by the first couple people who went through this material and have used the 12 steps to transcend their attachment to a personal ego while letting go of fears past and present. This book is partly a description of life currently from a mile-high viewpoint and partly an exploration of escalating levels of truth unfolding from page to page. This book was designed to deliver anyone who works through it from hell or mundanity experientially, to knowing more firsthand about the realities of heaven, as well as to aid a fellow traveler from traversing current parts of having heard about heaven to a more densely heavened life subjectively and experientially. This book was not created to be declarative in any way or made to force anyone to believe what's written within it. This book is a gift from the Holy Spirit to the world, and in the form of a guide for helping a spiritual traveler reach higher truths about God and the world they find themselves a part of.

This book is a jump-start of sorts for living spiritually and for the person seeking to have a relationship with divinity and the world around them in a more meaningful and personal way. This book was designed to deliver you a workable pathway for finding God in your own life and amongst your own community. This book was not created to replace the religion in your life or to convert you into the religion of another's choosing. This book is not religion nor does it claim to be, although there are scripture verses from four of the world's most enlightened religious figures: Christianity (Jesus), Hinduism (Krishna), Buddhism (The Buddha), Taoism (Lao Tzu). This book will not force you to believe anything, nor will it ask you to take any oaths or make any statements or pledges.

The design of this work of words is not to turn someone into angels over night or create a sense that enlightenment is possible for all those who work through these steps and who read these words, but what it will make a promise to do is deliver someone into upward stages of consciousness where the personal ego no longer holds total sway on what it is you think you are, or what it is you believe yourself to be.

The 12 steps, in and of themselves, have the power to deliver you to a handshake with divinity and to create a life where spirituality is lived and not just pretended to be practiced through whatever means seem popular at the time. This book has added commentary and context on the 12 steps for the purpose of expanding the steps into a ministry the whole world can take part in and find usefulness through. This book uses the steps in a recontextualized manner for the benefit of anyone who finds this work with the knowingness that you too will find immense value in working them, regardless of not being fortunate enough to have an active addiction to drugs or alcohol.

The way this book was put together is through the inspiration of a few who planted the idea for presenting the 12 steps as a collective good, not to be held only for the lucky few who find themselves addicts of one nature or another. This book is for everyone, regardless of you thinking you have a problem with your ego or not, for I have yet to meet a person who can control their thoughts and stop fears from arising, not to mention stop worry or shame, guilt, desire, cravingness, wantingness, attention, appreciation, or any other way the ego chooses to deliver awareness to you currently throughout your daily waking hours.

The personal ego is not something to be feared, nor is it something to be celebrated, at least not for the spiritual seeker. The ego for all people is what we think we are for the most part, until we're not anymore, and it's what's happening internally "for us" as opposed to "to us." The personal ego and the mind are the same thing, and both run wild with the imprinting of not only your youth, life, time on this earth, your parents, friends, schoolteachers, romantic partners, etc. etc., but also a means by which lifetimes of this imprinting has had a way to take place to produce what you currently believe to be a brain that allows stimulus to arise which you define as you. You are much more than what arises as thoughts, feelings or emotions. You are what witnesses such things, observes such things, allows for such things to be present by taking on human form. You are a degree of God manifested, not your thoughts, feelings, emotions, body, brain, wants and desires. If you don't know you're actually a locality of the omniscience of God, manifested into physicality for karmic reasons, then you have a problem with your ego and this book aims to help you with that as well as help alleviate all forms of fear in the process.

This book borrows truth from several places for the purpose of relaying their shared message together for the first time, without any personal agenda from the author, and all inspired by the Holy Spirit for the benefit of the reader and their community. This book presents you with truth on truth on truth on truth and weaved throughout is the story of the author as well as insights from the author on the truths found throughout history in varying religions and within the 12 steps themselves. This book is all truth, in varying degrees of intensity, compiled together to be the backstop for a truly transcendent spiritual life.

This book is the 12 steps, it is the shared truth of Jesus, Krishna, the Buddha and Lao Tzu. This book is a combination of so much truth that the reader's life will never be the same for just finding it, let alone finishing and doing the actual steps found within.

Lastly, this book is about you, about me, about our life together on this earth for millennia past and for the time present. This book holds no position politically or religiously, and it definitely doesn't intend on making the reader choose religion if they have none, or change someone's religious preference as a result of working through what's to come in the following pages.

...Why am I sharing this message?

At twenty years old, on the night described in a previous section where God showed up and answered my questions, I was told what my reason for being in human form was for this lifetime: I am to be a preacher unlike any other preacher, with a message unlike any other message.

The reason this message in book form is being shared is not because I'm better than another person, but because of the life that has been lived so far to deliver knowingness of God as the reality of existence. Because of my experience of life, I'm now ready to share with you the truth found along the way so that your life may see the same opportunity to manifest a genuine experience of God as real and as imminent. The moment God is no longer a wish or a hope to be true, but actually experienced in your own reality, your life will never be the same again. This book is a statement to the world that it's time to promote truth on a larger scale if I'm here to live out the answer from God as to why I'm here.

This book is not the only thing you should ever read to find out truths related to the Almighty, but this book is born out of the reality that I spent this lifetime chasing after the answers that have worked together to create the basis for this book, as well as the truth from a firsthand witnesser of the truth found within this book. Nothing within these pages is not from a place of experiential, witnessed, or observable lens. Nothing within this book is based on what someone else says about God as the merit for it being shared. Nothing in this book is based on anything other than a firsthand experience with divinity daily.

I was not ready to start a public ministry of the kind that is beginning with this title and others, as well as other creations taking shape, until I could speak authentically about a relationship with God that transcends even religion. I am not your pathway to God, this book is not the only pathway to God, as you yourself are already both without this work, even though you don't truly know that yet. This book's only aim is to remind you of something you already know but may have forgotten: God is everything, including you, not judging or condemning, always present waiting on your choice to experience the reality of ultimate truths.

I'm sharing this message because it's time to share this message, and because I'm here on this earth to share this message. Throughout my life, I would find worthy answers out in the world not from someone else relaying stories told by someone else or experienced by someone else at another time, but when someone spoke from their own experience. I found truth and lasting change when I stopped looking outside for the answers about God and started diving deeply into the internal being of what we all are, and from which answers came as a reflection of this pathway of surrender – which is what's shared here. This message and this book are truthful words strung together to deliver the reader from having to read about what someone may think to be true or what someone hopes is true, to a place of being witnessed experientially as true for themselves. If the work within this book had the power to deliver me from hell to Heaven in this world while still with a body, I know it has the same power in and of itself to do the same for you.

Because the same truth that I now witness is the same truth that all other beings of shared consciousness have witnessed, it is now time to speak about such truths in a dialogue fitting my story of shared realizations of God and how they came about. This book and its message are being shared because you need it on your journey of Self-discovery as much as I needed what's within it throughout my journey of discovering God as the Self.

...How did this book come to be?

As I was working through the 12 steps some years ago, I noticed life was changing rapidly. I found life was taking on a whole new definition of reality, and the life that was present each day was changing in a positive way with each new sunrise. As I continued to work through the steps in a formal fashion, I prayed and asked God to help me understand what was taking place from a spiritual and/or scientific standpoint.

Not long after that prayer, an author came into my awareness by the name of David R. Hawkins, in the form of his first book "Power vs. Force." As I made my way through its dialogue, I found that he also had lectures available online. In one lecture, he made reference to Byron Katie, or Byron Katie was made reference to by someone else within his lecture. I'm a little fuzzy on that part. But nevertheless, through a search for truth from David R. Hawkins, I found Byron Katie.

Hawkins's first book was a lot to take on at the time, but I knew the merit of it as soon as I started working through it. Once Byron Katie was brought up, something internally spoke to me to put Hawkins aside for a bit and find out what she was all about. I was on a golf course in Indiana when this moment arose and I immediately used audible.com to find her first book, "Loving What Is," downloaded it and hit play.

Katie's story is her own and I encourage anyone reading this to check out what she has to share with the world. What differentiates Katie's work from others is she created a model for running thoughts through almost an algorithm of sorts to ascertain their validity. As I put "the work" into practice, to my amazement, immediately what was realized is that my thoughts were mostly not true, and not only were they not true, but they weren't even asked to be thoughts in the first place. Meaning, I wasn't inviting them to arise or be present, but yet they still persisted as present and full of falsehood continually and without end.

As I continued doing what she calls "the work," I noticed that the thoughts were losing their strength and severity within my awareness, and that my attachment to them was letting go. Very quickly after realizing the truth that most of my thoughts were untrue representations of reality, the realization arose that I have thoughts but I'm not those thoughts. In quite a cascading fashion what came next was, I have a body but I'm not the body, followed by, I have a mind but I'm not the mind, and so on and so on until I was left without a direct attachment to everything I thought I was up until that point.

As I sat in silence with these new revelations, as well as within the confines of using AA as a model for moving past alcoholism, I was left with a question creating a new intent for life: If I'm not thoughts, not mind, and not the body… who and what am I?

As soon as this question crystalized, a stimulus arose within me to go back to Hawkins. Instead of finishing his first book as I spoke of before, I downloaded another of his offerings entitled "Letting Go."

As soon as I started listening to this book, I noticed that I was starting to have a contextual understanding of the changes taking place within my own life, which in turn was the completion of an answer to a prayer I had asked God about earlier. And so, I finished "Letting Go' and went back to 'Power vs. Force" and finished that up as well.

At the same time, once finishing "Letting Go," I shared the book with a dear friend, and to my amazement and delight, it was something he was searching for as well. We began a journey of self-discovery together and shared often our experiences of what was taking place in both of our lives as objective credence to the validity of the truth found within the book. Once I saw that it was just not anecdotal evidence of a change and miraculous things taking place just for me, I dove headfirst into the world and teachings of Dr. David R. Hawkins.

As my friendship grew with my fellow traveler discussing "Letting Go," and the effects it was having positively for both of us, I had an initial and faint urging from within to work on a book about the 12 steps for people who aren't suffering addictions to substances. As part of the continued discussions with my friend about "Letting Go," again finding myself on a golf course, he verbalized aloud what was already in my mind: "You should write a book about all of this happening to you and about the 12 steps in a format for everyone." And from that point forward I knew this book had to be written. I just didn't know the scope and angle of the actual work until recently.

This book was written because it arose out of a need to be written. This book was written because of the life changes taking place from working the 12 steps, realizations through the work of Byron Katie and Dr. Hawkins, and because someone else spoke out loud the need to have it completed which solidified an internal knowingness that a book of this kind would be beneficial.

I'll be eternally grateful for all the players in the play that led to the creation of this book, both the teachers I never met and the friend who inspired the final decision to put pen to paper and produce this final product.

...What is the personal ego?

From a spiritual sense and not from the Freudian world of therapy, a personal ego is what we all think we are ... until we're not. It's something we're born with, most die with, most are reborn with, and it's also the main way the individual believes they are separated from God while in the human form. It's a program that gets uploaded to the hardware of taking on the human body. The human brain acts as the processor of stimuli arising in and around the body, as well as the supercomputer which holds the body together and produces the experience of being in human form. The personal ego is the program for the brain like that of a computer operating system designed to allow for what comes next to work and have use.

The ego and the mind are the same thing. The brain doesn't have consciousness as a part of it, it only processes data, but consciousness is what gives the brain the ability to function as the computer and for the personal ego to be loaded onto it. Consciousness is the context out of which the mind has the ability to process content (think of it like the power source and source code). The personal ego is loaded as the primary awareness program for experiencing life somewhere during the lifecycle of being a baby within the womb. The personal ego is how people see the world around them. It is also what gets imprinted by everything seen and heard once arriving into the body. The mind in and of itself cannot tell truth from falsehood, as Hawkins so aptly puts it, and this is because the mind and the ego being the same thing only allow what's seen and heard to be downloaded into its programming, never rejecting what it sees as false or true, but instead downloading the stimuli as content without the experiencer ever being aware of such things taking place. The brain is run by electric impulses configured through neurotransmitters, with the mind's favorite fuel source being dopamine. Dopamine is the molecule of more, not the molecule of peace.

Most people believe they know if they're being lied to, but at the same time lie to themselves regularly. So how can we be sure what we're taking in via the world and media is true when we ourselves cannot stop lying even about the smallest things? How can we know truth from falsehood when the very brain we have to decipher stimuli (and its program, the mind) which allows anything in, don't work actively to limit falsehood from being uploaded? Meaning, we have a mind which is the experiential awareness program for the brain. But if we all remain in the belief that we are the brain or the mind, how can we know the truth through the brain when we're already programmed to be imprinted with everything that enters it without question? How can the mind innately know truth from falsehood when it believes itself to be God? If the mind innately knew truth from falsehood in a way that was useful, how is it that we still have war, famine, strife and conflict at every level of society? The mind is useful up to a point, and then woefully insufficient after that point.

The same logic goes for state-sponsored killing of people by a civilization claiming to be against murder. How can we stop murder if we kill legally? How can a society be against something while still being for it? Innately, the brain processes and stores what's imprinted on the mind, nothing more and nothing less. We can train the mind to operate within more of a logical or intellectual framework, but it's still just the mind allowing for different downloaded stimuli to be a result of imprinting and programming. Education sharpens the intellect and one's ability to logically deduce stimuli arising around them into quantifiable paradigms, but it only catalogues and regurgitates data presented overtime for one end or another.

We now have this thing called social media. If an observer of social media takes any time to look at how the mind and brain actually work, they'll see the exact thing they call being social, is the exact thing that causes anti-social behavior. As well as emotions and feelings to be present regardless if they believe their newsfeed is true or not. Our entire world of social media is nothing but false evidence appearing real, someone's opinion appearing valid, someone's voice being heard above another. Meaning, when someone uses social media, what they're really doing is constantly being imprinted with images and information that continue to keep them constantly being imprinted with more images and information. Regardless of the validity. Without social media, the January 6th insurrection in the United States would not have been possible.

What this does on a macro scale is not make the world a better place but puts the authority of a madman on the same page as the love of Mother Teresa. Equal weight between truth and falsehood creates a false equivalency, which in turn creates a world where the mind uploads falsity as much as truth. What the mind does with all of the falsehoods is not discard them from future use, it uses them as the basis for biases, feelings, emotions and stimuli for thoughts arising out of our control. You can't control the mind and one's thoughts, feelings and emotions by using the mind to do so. You have to surrender over the attachment to the ego and your beliefs that you are the mind in order to see it for what it is. The pathway to enlightenment is not found in controlling the mind, but instead found in surrendering over one's control of and attachment to it. Enlightenment and the mind are altogether different paradigms. For this same reason, science and religion can never prove or disprove the existence of God. The best they can do is point towards likelihoods and make statements about such possibilities.

Advertising works the same way as social media. If it didn't, why would companies use it as the primary way to have you buy things? You may be looking at a commercial for soap, which seems innocuous enough, but then the half-naked person starts lathering up with the soap as certain music and dialogue plays over top the ad, all designed to bypass reasoning and imprint a feeling when you see this particular soap again. Once you purchase the soap at the grocery store, now you're hooked for years to come. Not because you like the soap, but because the soap and sex are now imprinted as similar entities.

You think you know truth from falsehood. You truly want to believe that. But then you vote based on how you feel as opposed to who would protect America the best, or who would bring the most prosperity to your country of origin. Time and time again countries elect madmen to run their society, only to find out too late the lies were actually lies. The goal of the world is to create content for the individual, which is how the ego works. The ego doesn't care about you or how your life goes. It only does its job of producing attachments and aversions while continually moving forward for more of an opportunity to do so. It's a non-stop facilitator of positionality. God is this and that. But the mind is dead set on convincing you God is this *or* that. Causality is a byproduct of the mind, not present within the awareness of God.

The personal ego is not the bad guy. It is not to be feared, but instead should be approached with gratitude and hospitality. The personal ego, albeit the thing that seemingly separates the individual from God and the realizations of higher truths, is also the very same thing that shows the experiencer what should be surrendered over to find God again and again. The personal ego is both the thing that keeps mankind from knowing God experientially, and the same thing that shows mankind the way back to God through what needs to be surrendered.

The personal ego is not God. It's not even a god. But it's part of the spiritual traveler's experience while in human form, and because of this we needed to spend a little time going over the role and capacity of the ego/mind. Without looking at the mind first, there is no way to see it for what it is.

In this personal experience of life this time around, were it not for the personal ego, I would have been born knowing God without the choice to choose knowing God. If this place, this world and this realm were designed to know God without interruption, there would not be an ego nor be a human body to go along with it. But this world is not designed to be an unabated reality of the truth of God. It is designed to be a place where we get to choose God and work off the karma of lives lived before and now.

The reason we have this book is so we can transcend our attachment to the mind and finally experience God as if it was for the first time while still carrying these bones around. We breakdown the hold the ego has on us by practicing surrender, and it's only through surrender, forgiveness and gratitude do we win the prize of freedom. The funny thing is, once someone is free from the ego altogether at the highest levels of consciousness, which is a rare reality on this planet, the vision from that viewpoint shows that neither the ego nor the person is ever apart or outside of God to begin with. The illusion and belief of separateness vanishes altogether the moment enlightenment sets in. The experiencer turns from being what we think we are to being more and more of the witnesser at the level of unconditional love. But it's not until Satcitananda (the beginning of enlightenment unfolding) sets in that one has transcended all attachment to the personal ego in rapid succession. And it's not until a high level of enlightenment does the personal ego cease to exist in all totality.

The personal ego is part and parcel of the human experience until it isn't any longer. Within the ego we have not just what the world would characterize as bad things or negative things, in all actuality, the ego can be quite beneficial to mankind. The intellect is an active component of the ego's build and make-up, which has been a significant source and positive aspect of growth for the human species. Within the workings of the ego there is the ability to take credit for inspiration and motivation, but when taken as a whole, the ego is not to be feared, fought against, beaten down, or looked poorly upon, but instead understood first and surrendered over eventually. The only way to God is going through the mind, but one won't find God without surrendering over attachment to the belief they are the mind.

The fastest way to see the glory and splendor of God shine brilliantly upon your face is to let go of the beliefs that your mind is important or that your thoughts mean anything. It is possible to be in the world but not of it, but only once surrender becomes part of what you are. As long as you believe you're your thoughts, feelings and emotions, you're attached to this world and have to be in it and of it.

The ego is cunning and adventurous, not to mention smart and capable of pretending to be god. Humility/surrender is the key to aid in the disillusion of the personal ego, followed by forgiveness and gratitude. The quickest way to find relief from aspects of the painful moments with ego is to serve God by serving someone else. If you want to get away from the chaos of your mind the fastest, go help someone by loving them in whatever means presents itself.

...What is fear?

There are all kinds of valuable acronyms for fear, with possibly the most apt being "False Evidence Appearing Real."

Fear has many forms, but the best way to recognize fear is as anything which isn't the direct experience, witness or observation of love. Or as anything which brings about confusion in any form.

I'm not speaking of confusion related to learning a new language or in the aspect of education. I'm referring to confusion within the aspect of life where decision making becomes paramount, but one is unable to see a clear direction. As an example: You are a salesman and you have been asked to compromise integrity by not telling the whole truth to a group of perspective clients about the actual completion date for the product you're selling. Because of this moment, it causes you pain around having an upcoming meeting and causes anxiety about what you should do. On one hand, you have a good paying job that is often better than worse, and if you didn't have this job, you'd have to find another one to replace it, but maybe in this atmosphere of job searching, that feels like a struggle. Without this job you may get behind on bills and because of this you believe your significant other could leave you. What is a person supposed to see in this example? False evidence appearing real.

The falsity arises within the confusion about what to do in the upcoming meeting. Fear is littered throughout this example as a means of showing how fear is not being scared for your life, although that could be a byproduct of fear, but more of the insidious nature of life with regards to shame, guilt, resentments, anger, depression, wantingness, cravingness, remorse, desiring something, and so on and so on. Without a central pillar of integrity and the practiced gift of surrender, it would be easy to see that a little lie would serve all parties equally. That's just how business is done you tell yourself, because the product will eventually be ready. Right?

Fear of the past is called worry or regret or guilt, while fear of the future is generally called anxiety. Byron Katie's work on this subject is a quality way to work through fears as well, but for the sake of this writing, what needs to be seen is that fear is an aspect of the ego. And it's a lower aspect of the ego that keeps people separated from love most often, but at the end of the day does very little to create balance or harmony in anyone's life. Fear, like thoughts, is not what you are but more like what you have to walk through. Fear is fake, not real, physically not a thing, an illusion. However, it may feel real, but only as real as you believe feelings to be.

What if the person in our example decides to tell their boss they won't lie for the company as asked to? What happens if that person gets fired over not lying? And what happens if the partner leaves this person over losing their job? Does any of that matter in the long run? Is that job worth having if you're paid to lie? Is that person worth having in your life if they leave you over having morals and principles? And is the fear of not getting another job justified based on just the anxiety over what the job market might look like for you?

I have been poor and dead broke, two similar but altogether different things. Depending on when you've known me, being poor or being broke was either a curse or one of the greatest blessings of my life. I have had the great opportunity of having not a single dollar to my name many times and still all my needs were provided by God, from random people offering me dinner, to finding money needed for gas, to having a roof over my head provided. I can attest to the fact that despite the amount of money in my bank account, I have neither starved nor not been able to get another job, have a place to stay or clothes to wear.

Fear is always based on shaky ground, for it's in our head that fear has the opportunity to take hold, within the same mind that doesn't know truth from falsehood, but rarely in life does fear have any merit about the situation at hand. Unless it arises as a foreboding measure for what another is experiencing or what might be on the horizon. But even then, it's not worth holding onto as absolute truth. What happens if we fear for our life because of a situation we find ourselves a part of, let's say a robbery or a standoff with police we're in the middle of? Is fear worth holding onto as a reality in these situations as well? And will it help you think better or be more ready for decisions to be made? What if you get shot or die? Is dying worth fearing if everyone has to do it at some point? Is the possible pain in the future of being shot worth agonizing about in the present before it happens? Or better yet, worth agonizing about it being a possibility in the future?

I have yet to find a time when fear of anything saved me from a situation I needed saving from. Trust in God in times of distress and surrender over all fears to the creator when they arise, and if you do this you'll be amazed at how puny and insignificant fear really is.

The fastest way to dismantle fear is by looking at it head on and walking through the hail of bullets it presents, while continually surrendering over your attachment to the experience of it. What you'll find when you do this as opposed to when you cower and hide from it, is that you'll either die physically and open your eyes still in existence but separate from the body and surrounded by love. Or, you move through a difficult situation unscathed and better for the experience next time.

Fear is an innately cowardly feeling, and not something that surrender and prayer can't remedy. Why spend your life in fear another day when love stands waiting just on the other side of walking through it? Your true Self is a characteristic and aspect of the Alpha and the Omega, and because of this, in all actuality, fear is like a pebble in front of you. With the pebble, one can either kick it around and play with it for a while, eventually even picking it up and putting it in your pocket and calling it mine, or you can politely step over it and continue on your way. A pebble is just a pebble, and a fear is just fear — both are small and part of life, but once you call it mine, they take on new significance and meaning.

At the root of all fear, you'll find the fear of death waiting to be surrendered. What happens when you surrender over your attachment to life and your unwillingness to expire? What happens is you find peace and love waiting for you at the end of the equation. Again, fear doesn't lead to death. It's only a pebble. For our time is appointed to be born and to die but fear most assuredly leads to the blocking off of love in your life in the meantime. And it becomes part of the decision-making process when one is separated from a willingness to trust that God sees you and what you're going through.

Fear produces confusion, whereas love produces clarity.

Fear produces war, love produces peace.

Fear produces "us against them" and love produces "us and them."

The mind fears what it believes is different from its host, whereas love transcends the mind and makes apparent that the host body is nothing more than a temporary way to choose love over fear.

...How are fear and ego related?

When looking at the ego/mind, we can use an image to describe the relationship between fear in all its forms and the ego/mind, with that imagery being a coin. The coin is the mind, with one side interaction with the content of the world and the other side thoughts, feelings and emotions. As one flips the coin up from their fingertips it spins effortlessly in the air, blending both the interaction with the world and thoughts, feelings and emotions seemingly together and without end, until the coin comes back down to lie still on the hand waiting for another flick in the air.

Every moment of choice allows the person flipping the coin to either look at it for what it is while lying still in the hand, or to watch the coin spin effortlessly up in the air once more after choosing to flick it. The coin neither cares what direction you flip it, nor does it care how many rotations it makes. The coin is just being a coin, regardless of how you spin it. The more you see yourself as the coin in the air the more hypnotized you become by it.

Fear and the ego are also like a TV, where the viewer can turn it on and start flipping through channels without having a desired television station or program to land on. As one flips through the channels the TV remains the TV, but the channels either get stopped and watched or passed by for something else. Either way, the channel is still just a channel and the TV is still just a TV. What station the viewer decides to land on and continue watching is not the fault of the TV or the channel broadcasting. Fear arises within the ego, but the ego and fear are not precisely the same thing. Fear is a program which is viewable through the mind, but the mind is not the creator of the program, it just allows it to play as long as the viewer chooses to watch it.

Fears, however, are some of the most potent weapons the ego has at its disposal for survival. Fears allow the experiencer the false belief that they are the ego, because when fear is present it feels real and confronting. Fear is what keeps people trapped in lifetimes of oppression, because fear is false evidence appearing real. What's real is not the fear, what's real is the consciousness allowing fear to be present in the first place. Not unlike the viewer from above, you're not the TV nor the coin flipping in the air, you're what is watching both be part of existence. Fear seems powerful because it bypasses thoughts almost immediately and presents itself as a feeling or an emotion, which in reality are just conglomerates of un-surrendered thoughts imprinted over eons of time.

Thoughts build into feelings. Many uninvestigated feelings cement into emotions, and once an emotional set is complete, the severity of the fear feels more real because it has been flipped up in the air so many times, the person flipping the coin forgets that the person flipping, and the coin, are not the same thing, and that watching TV, when all is said and done, is just a waste of time.

...How does my level of consciousness affect my surroundings?

One's level of consciousness informs the entire way they view themselves, God, the world around them, and their beliefs about life. We are all born with a calibrated level of consciousness, and we all have an opportunity to evolve or devolve on that same scale throughout our time with a body. The higher one's level of consciousness the more love one feels, and the lower the level of consciousness the less.

At a certain point in this journey, I asked God for a definition I could understand as to what we all are and what this entire life was around me. What I got as an answer was: I, in greater or lesser degrees of intensity.

Then I asked what the intensity was referring to and the answer was Love. And Truth.

From the moment in time when I was twenty years old and God showed up in a way I never experienced before, what showed up all around me was not religion, or religious figures, or fear in any form. What showed up was Love, with the energy of Love bringing and being the knowingness in that moment that God is Love, not in totality, but in how we experience the reality of God. What was made clear moving forward from that day was not that God is found in a religion, but that God is found in love. So, the way we experience God is through love, varying degrees of it. Love is another way of saying the energy of God, or the awareness of God present. The way we know God is because of love, and the way we're saved from ourselves is because of Love.

The way this world works is through vibrations of energy manifested as content and awareness of content. Out of the awareness of content and because of Love, we have what's called context, which all content arises out of. Content is not apart from context, but because of context and because all context is God, content has the opportunity to arise into physicality as an aspect of that from which it arose. Hence, "I, in greater or lesser degrees of intensity."

What you are draws to you what you need in order to be that or to move past that. Righteous actions fueled by righteous intent create an upward momentum towards experiencing and eventually being more and more love, until one arrives at being love, or unconditional love, or something far greater than even those two wonderful gifts. Someone who is perfected love, meaning having no barriers to the knowingness that what they are is Love and Love is all they are, can best be seen in the western world as Jesus the Christ. Someone we can look to as being all lower mind, or slave to ego, would be someone in history who took it upon themselves to try and get rid of an entire species of a race known as Jews. From someone who was all Love, the world found hope and peace subjectively for many, but from someone who was all fear and far from knowing Love, the world found devastation and torment.

Most people fall somewhere in between not knowing Love and thinking they're their mind. The intensity from which you experience the reality and truth of "I" is what dictates your entire life and what you'll experience to be true and real. One's perception is entirely contingent upon their level of "I-ness." When you have time, feel free to look at Dr. David R. Hawkins's map of the scale of consciousness, and you'll see how it works in this world at this time. For a quick reference, a couple sections down, I have included aspects of his scale of consciousness designed to be separate from his work but show in a small way how Love manifests in an upward trajectory.

Consciousness is another word for Omniscience, which is one of the three descriptors' religions use to define God. Omniscience is an aspect of God as knowing everything. Our calibrated level of consciousness is how we know something as opposed to just understanding it. Have you ever had an "ah-ha" moment? Everyone has, but few know what's happening when these take place.

Whenever someone has an "ah-ha" moment, what's happening is they are experiencing higher degrees of truth, which recontextualize the entirety of what was known before the moment. What that moment is in reality is their consciousness flipping and evolving towards more knowingness, an evolution and upwards progression towards being more Love than they were prior. "Ah-ha" moments are glimpses into the field of consciousness from a higher level of knowingness than just previously held. As one moves into the world of being love or above in Hawkins' scale of consciousness, the "ah-ha" moment becomes more and more regular as the state of one's current level of existence increases towards being a constant awareness of "ah-ha" moments. Meaning, the more truth we become, the more intense our "I-ness" becomes, which in turn creates more love present for your experience in this body as well as for the world's experience of you in that body.

What we all are is nothing more than that which witnesses the nature and reality of that which created the ability to witness. We're all localities of consciousness, expressed as what we know to be love, but in all reality, love is just how we experience God, until at a certain point one moves away from momentary experiences of God and realizes they are God, which creates a subjective experience of life where one becomes the "ah-ha" moment full time.

As one moves upward in their level of consciousness, they allow for more love to be present, and when more love is present, life changes dramatically every time. Likewise, as one's level of consciousness moves downward, less love is felt as present, which makes the experiencer feel less connected to divinity, and more a part of the world. When one is fully a part of the world and cut off from the sunlight of the Spirit, they serve the world and look to the world for happiness and hope. When one becomes a slave to the ego, under a certain level of consciousness, which many on this planet find themselves, they have no idea what they are in reality, and believe their only hope for survival is taking and not giving. Hope outside of Love is like works without action, futile. Love equals abundance, whereas the lack of love equals the belief that abundance is a myth.

This book is not designed to be a full explanation into the world of consciousness. This book was created to move someone through the 12-steps so they can have their own experience with Truth. If you have a desire to go deeper into the levels of consciousness, which is recommended for anyone desiring to do so, it's best to start being exposed to Dr. David R. Hawkins's work, and I would recommend starting with what he wrote and spoke when alive and not what has been published posthumously, starting with his first book Power vs. Force. This work will lay a solid foundation as to what his discoveries are and what they mean for humanity and for your life specifically. This book does not depend on Dr. Hawkins and his Map of Consciousness. We simply use it as a short hand to demonstrate the levels of humanity that a spiritual traveler will traverse on their journey.

With regards to the mention of consciousness here, we do it for a reference to language and as a building block of truth used to see the ego for what it truly is – not as a complete summation of consciousness research.

...How does my ego/fear stop me from getting what I desire most?

This is an interesting question because the word "desire" is what needs to be elaborated on in more detail. "What we desire" is a phrase many people use, but what they mean by desire is "want." I used to believe that proper language was important for bringing about in my life what was most wanted, and I thought that if I used the word "desire," somehow that word had more power and less negativity than "want." So, I would let the universe know my desires repeatedly, thinking that if I desired something enough it would magically manifest as in the book The Secret. That's not how God works and that's not how life works. The ego desires and wants and puts expectations on things, whereas love lets go of desires and wants and attachments and expectations. We all desire something for a certain time, and then some of us realize that the act of wanting is the only payoff to having desires. The attachments to our desires and wants bring suffering, the letting go of our attachments and wants brings about joy.

We don't magically will something into existence through wanting or desiring it. Desire works best if one surrenders it over for a preference about life, and then, in turn, surrenders over that preference becoming an outcome as well. You draw to you what you need, not what you want. When we desire something, we're saying that we need something to be something we're not, whether that is to be happy or feel complete, but in all reality what we are is already complete regardless of desires. We just don't see that yet because of our current level of consciousness.

What you are and what you have is all you need and all you can handle at the current moment, for if it wasn't, more would be present. If you look around and find yourself wanting something, this is a good place to start asking God why it is you want that thing. And why getting it would fix something that isn't broken to start with. We always have everything we need to be something in the future we're currently not, that's how Life works. Whatever we need to evolve consciously is already in our possession, and as one moves upwards through the scale of consciousness, more abundance becomes pronounced in physicality, because what you are has evolved into more abundance and what you needed to reach that point has presented itself to you as always with you. We don't manifest wealth by desiring wealth and wanting wealth. For spiritual travelers, wealth either comes as a result of what you need to be more of you than what's present, or it doesn't come to you because wealth is not something needed.

The reason it appears that wealth arrives to those who are bad people more than to those who are good people, is because we're all here for different reasons, and karmically, maybe wealth isn't in your card this time around and it is for another, regardless of their level of consciousness. However, wealth isn't a sign of God's feelings towards you one way or another – you're not favored by God because you have money, no matter what prosperity gospel preachers tell you. You can't serve two masters equally, so if you desire to be rich above all else, this book is not for you, but I wish you the best of luck in your pursuits. In my experience, however, I have never had more wealth than when I surrendered over all attachment to money, and because of not desiring wealth, when it arises, I act as just a pass-through of it for the world around me. If you desire wealth in this lifetime, surrender over that desire completely. Once all attachment to attaining wealth is let go, watch how fast you become someone who the world sees as wealthy.

If you desire to serve the world by being a part of the world this time around, by all means do so, and you will even find it easier to acquire more gold and jewels than most, but what you will never find is satiation, lasting happiness, joy and internal peace. However, if your intent is to know God, let go of your desires and wants and allow God to bring more truth into your life. And if the byproduct of more truth is more wealth, or a partner in life, then give thanks to God for it. And if those things never arise as a result of growing closer to God, give thanks for that as well. We always have exactly what's needed to grow closer to God or move further away from truth, the only difference between the two is perspective.

If we go back strictly to the question at hand, "How does ego/fear stop me from getting what I desire most?" and approach this question from another angle, we first have to define what's desired most. For the vast majority of my early life, I desired to know the truth about Life above all things. Along the way, fear stopped me from seeing Love time and time again, because I believed I was what I felt or my emotions and thoughts arising from moment to moment. If your desire is to know God and to find happiness, it all boils down to how willing you are to let go of your attachments to fears and worries, because if you're not willing to have faith in what's found at the end of a surrender process, then fear is definitely a block to your pursuits. If what you want most is to transcend the ego and let go of all attachments to fear in all its forms, but you're not willing to have faith that surrendering over your attachment to the juice your ego gets by holding onto the residue of being wronged and/or feeling superior to others, then what you desire most is blocked once again. According to the Buddha, attachments and aversions are the root of all pain and suffering, meaning, the longer you stay attached to how you're feeling as being what you are, or the longer you have an aversion to surrendering your attachment to experiencing an aspect of life we call fear, suffering will continue to exist as your reality. Desires and cravings left to their own devices will lead the person down a road of more desires and cravings, never to a road that ends with satisfaction.

In order to grow closer to truth, and in turn closer to God, serving two masters is something you have to understand and then know innately the truth of. Desiring wealth or a significant other, or for a particular miracle to arise in your life is not a bad thing, it's simply a block in a wall you're building in front of ever attaining that thing. The truth is, when you need something to evolve or to better prove the example of what you are to the world, you'll have it. And if you don't need something to be more of that which you already are through worldly displays of what you are, you won't have it. Either way, desiring something doesn't help it manifest into physicality. Actually, it is quite the opposite.

...What are the levels of consciousness and how do they correspond with my happiness?

Higher Levels of **Enlightenment**
Enlightenment through **Victorious Peace**
Joy
Love
Reason
Acceptance
Willingness
Neutrality
Courage
Pride
Anger
Desire
Fear
Grief
Apathy
Guilt
Shame

The levels of consciousness above are a representation of the non-linear world manifesting as comprehensible content. The levels of consciousness comprised above were established by Dr. David R. Hawkins and are not of my own making. I only lovingly use aspects of his chart and the levels above as a means of consciousness shorthand within this book for the purpose of having something easy to reference back to, for both the reader and the author. More information on the map of consciousness and all of the priceless consciousness research done by Dr. Hawkins over the long and extraordinary life that he lived, can be found by doing any Google search or by picking up one of his many books, all of which go into consciousness in more detail than this particular book will.

The levels of consciousness are direct indicators of one's current perception and interaction with the world, derived through an understanding that the non-linear (spirit) is as much of the linear (physicality) as Love is a characteristic of God. And as far as happiness goes, in relation to the levels of consciousness, one can see from the map that those calibrated levels of courage and above are marked in bold, showing that more and more happiness presents itself as a byproduct only when someone inhabits a consciousness level of courage or higher. Happiness can be experienced in starts and fits within the lower consciousness levels, but most commonly does not last in any meaningful way until someone reaches a level of courage or above.

Statistical certitude shows me that some of you reading this book will not be operating from a level of courage or above. But quite possibly many of you reading this book were brought to the work precisely because you have a need that brought this text to you for the expressed purpose of helping you reach the level necessary to transform your life for the better. Another possibility for this work being brought to your attention is that you have enough positive karma to draw it into your life for the purpose of helping you move from a positive state to a loving state. Or even beyond. Or a third explanation for finding this material is that you have reached your end and find yourself not wanting to wake up tomorrow, like where I found myself, but aren't yet willing to pull the final trigger.

Regardless, this book has arrived in your hour of need, as the levels of consciousness arrived at mine. At the consciousness level of courage, the experiencer first begins to realize there is something greater from which it was hatched. The etheric brain begins to take shape allowing for group karma to dissipate as a means of existing and individual karma to come forth. Did you ever see a flock of birds, maybe hundreds of them, flying in the same direction at the same time and all of a sudden, they all turn, and turn again, and land in the same place and take off at the same time in the same direction? Well, when you are operating below a level of courage, unknowingly, you are doing the exact same thing as the birds. When you move from a group karma to an individual karma, you have been given the gift to evolve personally. When you cross over into courage it is like there is an internal compass that's now present that wasn't before. With this compass pointing you in the direction of more and more truth instead of less and less of it. Courage is the demarcation line of an entirely different life from what lies below it.

There are several different methods for calibrating one's level of consciousness, and I will leave that research up to you to do on your own if curiosity so informs your intent. For the purpose of this book, however, it is not necessary to know where you fall along the levels of consciousness. What is necessary is making your way through the rest of our dialogue and applying the spiritual principles when and where applicable. By doing this, I assure you that happiness will be an allowable way of life for you.

The most basic aspect of life is beingness. And wherever your journey has taken you so far it managed to deliver you to this work in order to help you learn again what you already know and have only forgotten. This book delivers you to you, but without illusion attached. This work is designed to aid a person in their journey towards freedom from the ego. But another beautiful byproduct of what you're currently reading today is that it will help you feel better just because of the field it creates for the reader while reading it. If you have found this book and you're still reading at this point, understand that you can choose from here on to either pursue enlightenment in this lifetime, or not, with the aid of this text, but what will happen without you even realizing it, is that your life will start changing the moment you decide to work this program for yourself.

One piece of advice I will give at this point is that if you start this work and your life becomes suddenly more chaotic, don't stop doing the work, because that means it's working fast. Don't forget, all fear is an illusion – it's safe to continue straight ahead no matter what. The moment you start this work, the ego will know its days as master are numbered, and because of that fact, there's no telling what illusory dramas await your experience in the days, weeks, months, and years ahead. As you're faced with another challenge, hardship, hurdle, or stressor which tells you to put the work down and give up on knowing God, in that moment you'll have the choice to walk straight ahead through fear or succumb to it and remain stagnant.

The very act of life changing all around you is the proof that what you're doing is having an effect. Surrender is the ultimate tool that underlies this entire book. And I would be misleading you if I didn't warn you that once you make advancements towards love through surrender, fear is closely behind working to stop you from experiencing what's just beyond your line of sight. If you have this book in your hands, you've already made the decision not to kill yourself, or give up on happiness, and as you cross over into the land of courage if you're not already there, or as you elevate consciously upward from the level you currently reside in, be ready for one "ah-ha" moment after another. What is written here is already known by you and has already been stated throughout the halls of time, but to be sure it's beyond clear where the credit for this work comes from, I point lovingly back to how it will become nothing more than a tool you use to remember what you already know.

The heavens are not above you, they are within you. Because of that you're already everything you'll ever need in order to realize and then embrace your life with an attitude of, "Okay God, where shall we go from here?"

"Ah ha" moments are tidbits of seeing through the illusion of life and simultaneously remembering you already knew what just a moment ago was perceived as unknown. Truth is not for sale. It is not hidden for later purchase. It does not have dues or fees. You can't pay for a weekend conference full of it and expect it to stick. It's that truth only appears when we're karmically ready for it to, and never before. And never because we expected it, manipulated someone for it, or think we've found it through anything other than being exactly who we are as we experience it. There is a time to reap and a time to sow, and this book is an aid in that truth. For maybe holding this book in your hands now is because your life is about to sprout. Or maybe it's because the truth found within these pages are only meant at this time to plant seeds of understanding. Either way, you're on the right path by even reading these words and knowing this book exists.

The levels of consciousness from one aspect are nothing more than an illustration of the omniscience of God and how divinity manifests consciously in each and every one of us. From another aspect, the levels of consciousness are how happiness is guaranteed, and how transcending the ego and fear in all its forms is plausible. The scale of consciousness is not something I created. Again, it must be stated, if you desire to know more, do your own research. Their representation here is nothing more than a way to create a backdrop for what will take place as you work through this book and carry your message of love out into the world.

By working the 12 steps found within this book, you'll not only witness a change happen in your life for the positive, but you will grow closer to God and be filled with more love than you have ever felt to date. As was stated previously in the answer to this question, if you continue into the work of this book and start the steps, not only is freedom guaranteed through your authenticity and intent to know God, but chaos will become present as well. For when you decide that happiness is your path and knowing God is your choice, the ego as part of how it works, goes into overdrive to bring forth everything you've ever been stuck to or attached to or believed throughout millennia. Choosing God, means that which you're not will present itself for the purpose of giving you what's needed to grow closer to God. Again, whatever is needed is provided, because you can't just desire your way to God. You have to choose to walk toward God deliberately.

...Why should I care about raising my level of consciousness and transcending the ego and fear?

The answer to the question is simple: raising one's level of consciousness is directly correlated to the amount of love and happiness present in your life. Period.

There are no secrets under heaven about the way of God and the way of the world. All one has to do to know about either is open their eyes in an honest fashion and take in the sights and sounds of both. There are no secrets you'll find from mystics beyond the grave who claim to have wisdom worth channeling that will deliver the spiritual aspirant into an actual experience of regular, subjective joy and happiness other than the truth found within the answer to the question of this section. The only way to God is up, and the only way to misery and pain is down. There are no mysteries to experiencing God that are left undiscovered, and all of the enlightened sages of old will agree with the logic in this next statement: God is not somewhere else waiting in judgment of what's here and now; God is right here now, waiting on your interaction with consciousness to recognize such.

It matters little if you agree with what's been stated here. The only thing that matters is having your own subjective experience with God. That experience is within you and always possible. It is never dependent upon someone else telling you what to do, or claiming to be the bridge you need. False prophets and false teachers equating your journey to God with the amount of money you are willing to part with are not the answer and never were. You cannot buy your way to God.

This book is simple, straightforward, holds no punches, delivers only truth, and was written so that you as the spiritual seeker and world traveler have the same opportunity I did: to see God for yourself, to choose God for yourself, and to know firsthand the reality that shines bright for the author of these words today.

Hell is not a place to find oneself in, with this body or without this body. Likewise, heaven is but a choice away for this life and for the next lifetime to follow. The quickest way to preserving a spot in heaven once out of this body is by accepting Jesus as your savior, but the quickest way to experiencing heaven while in this body is by being a living example of Jesus through surrender, forgiveness, and gratitude.

The gifts of surrender, forgiveness and gratitude practiced regularly for yourself and the world around you is the only recipe needed to raise your level of consciousness and transcend fear in all its forms. To live like Jesus is as simple as practicing these three gifts from God, all the time, everywhere. No matter what.

...How can this book help me live the life I have always dreamed of?

I can't put words in your mouth. So, today I'll describe the life I always dreamed of and do my best to describe how it came to be experientially. With all of this information, you can decide for yourself if this book will help create the same opportunity to have a life of dreams fulfilled for you as well.

I wanted happiness as a child and adolescent, young adult, and early adult. I wanted to know God was real, and I wanted to be sure that this life had more merit to it than just existing to acquire goods and possessions. I wanted truth at all costs and was willing to go to the ends of the earth to find it. I desired hope and joy as real experiences of lasting significance as opposed to momentary spots of enjoyment. I prayed for a way to God that made sense and was born out of experience rather than taking someone else's word for it. I wanted love and to be loved and to give love without selfishness. I wanted a firsthand experience of the creator that I was able to witness and able to hold as truth. I wanted a connection with God more than anything on this earth, a connection which allowed me to know what the highest will of God was for my life as opposed to just going through the motions of working a job for the sake of working a job. I wanted the truth of God above all else, and nothing but the direct experience of such provided validity for living.

On July 4th, 2017, as well as twelve years prior at twenty years of age, a series of events were set in motion where I knew God existed but didn't know what to do with that information and experiential knowledge. At twenty, I came face to face with divinity through the gift of an overwhelming experience, and at thirty-two I came face to face with divinity again through the gift of regained sanity. And both times I had my answer about God being real. For twelve years, following the experience at twenty, I went out into the world and tried to live two lives simultaneously, one of the world and one of knowing the truth about the reality of God. The world chewed me up and spit me out and delivered me straight to hell. At twenty, I knew the truth but didn't act on the truth, and I had truth but didn't know what to do with truth. At thirty-two, when presented with another moment of the reality of God being present beyond words and description other than to say that sanity was a by-product, I chose another way to live from twelve years prior – I chose to move away from the world and towards truth found within and not found out in the world of the ego. This book is an account of the years since choosing another way to live and another way to embrace the reality of God. This book is the source of information about my particular journey this time around which led to the realization of God as Self, and as all that is, all that was, and all that ever will be. All experienceable while with this body because of the gift of grace, as well as out of this body through the never-ending gift of grace.

Today, life has never been sweeter. Today, life has never had more meaning and significance. Today, my life is not my own nor will it ever be again. Today, heaven is a reality while on earth as much as it is a reality when these mortal coils are shed for good. Today, who I am is a person free of attachments. Attachments to wanting, attachments to cravings, attachments to desiring, attachments to aversions, attachments to opinions, attachments to resentments, attachments to suffering. Today, I know what I didn't know before, that I am not the mind, not the body, and not the ego. And neither are you.

The veil has been pulled back and the Glory of God regularly shines through in ways unbelievable to most, and experienceable by few. The belief by many is this subjective experience is only for the few or doesn't actually have the ability to exist at all. Today, I am the example of doing what Christ did in order to have a connection with God as Christ did. Today, I don't choose to be separated from the spirit of God through choosing the world. Today, the world is but a television set where the dramas of the ego play out as something aside from the ultimate reality of truth. Today, there is no causality or duality, there is only I. Along this journey there have been no "others," telling me what to do next or instructing me on the reality of God. There has just been an internal knowingness always elevating in its ability to grow louder and louder through consciousness as to what choice can be made next. In your journey to God, you will not rely on someone else as the means to coming face-to-face with Truth. You will only have aids, like this book, which are used to point you in the direction you must walk for yourself. If you find someone on your pathway to God who says you need them to find God, politely walk past their offer of help and keep straight and narrow on the path of righteousness.

I am on this earth this time around to be a witness to the teachings of many but the life of one: Jesus. I am not here to be Jesus or to claim the authority of Jesus, but I am here nonetheless to tell the world through actions that if you desire a life worth living, a life worth experiencing, and a life worth sharing effortlessly with the world, do as I did, chase after God as I did, but let go of your attachment to the world sooner than I did and heed these words: Jesus was Love personified in the human form; Love lived out as an example for everyone to follow; Love given as grace to those too weary to travel the spiritual path towards higher truths; and Love which can be emulated and lead to the final doorway of enlightenment. The only way to find true happiness is to surrender over all that you are attached to about how one defines themselves as separate from the rest, apart from God, without the need for an example and savior like Jesus, and who have too little humility to admit that they are not God, but only ego gods until they aren't any longer.

If you are not willing to humble yourself before the creator and ask for help with finding truth and working through this book, this work is not for you, and a truly spiritual life may not be for you. But also, lasting happiness may not be for you. However, just because chasing after God with a reckless abandon may not be for you this time around, that doesn't mean it won't be next time or at another point in the future.

I am sharing this entire message with you so that what becomes abundantly clear by the end of it – if a sinner like what the world knows as Mason can have the life that's present today, so can you. Don't follow me as someone who asks for your devotion, don't follow me at all, just follow my lead toward God and know that because I did it so can you. And because I did it and lived to tell the tale, it's a safe pathway to travel toward finding God in your life as something real and not made up.

If you want a life like what was described above, this book is for you. A surrendered life is for you. A lasting and known connection with God is for you. Humility to accept the example of Jesus is for you. The wisdom to see truth in the Masters of old is for you. And the journey you can take to get there can start for you right now, here, if you choose to read.

Again, it must be stated: you will never find God because another person allows you to do so, because another person shares certain secrets with you, or because you reach a higher level within a program which costs money or requires oaths. God is right here, right now, free of cost, always present, always loving, always God. All you have to do to realize God as imminent is to choose faith in the moments when fear is present, and choose faith by walking straight ahead through the hail of bullets no matter what, choosing to find God no matter what, no matter the time it takes, and no matter the obstacles in your way.

SECTION ONE

\-

Chapters 1 - 3

\-

Surrender

Chapter 1

TRANSCENDING THE FORCES OF SHAME & GUILT

Powerlessness and unmanageability pretty much summed me up…

It wasn't so long ago that shame and guilt were part of my regular experience of being human. For years, I made decisions which did not bring me closer to God. I became cognizant that every interaction in life is a choice to choose God or not. But I continued to make choices that reinforced my continuing sense of shame and guilt. Shame, guilt, and other forms of fear create perpetual loops of choosing and then believing you are the thing you just chose. When you choose something over and over again it turns into a belief system about yourself and all your worth being dictated by the outcomes of the same decisions. That you are shame. That you are guilt. The truth is, you are neither.

For 32 years, I was a lost man. I continually pursued answers about life out in the world. And searched for such answers amongst those who also searched for truth in low down and far-off places – without satisfaction ever being part of the equation. I would search for the meaning of love by lusting after people. I would search for the meaning of money by falsely claiming work done as worth a day's wage. I would look for friendship in frivolity and regularly drink myself into oblivion. The plain and simple truth about me for many years was that I didn't even like being alive most of the time. I hated being me.

I was constantly hiding from God in places I thought would be good enough to appease God. I would make deals and I would barter with divinity about choices once made to never be made again. Only to repeat the same negative choices all over. I would cower from responsibility and run from commitment, only to continue these patterns. What a bare laden carcass of a man I was by the time I reached the age of thirty-two. There was a falsehood I couldn't get out of the way of, which was in order to embrace a calling shared with me at 20, I had to be Jesus for everyone. When the truth all along was that I simply have to show the world I know Jesus, not through words but solely through actions. The frustration that was mounting was that I didn't know Jesus either. Not from a first-hand perspective. I also no longer believed in the religion of Christianity to show me who or what God was.

I peddled in half-truths and outright lies. And for the most part I pretended to be what I thought others wanted me to be. I spent years telling someone I loved them only to burn that bridge through deliberate acts of self-destruction in a twisted attempt to have them prove their love to me in return by not leaving me when I was worth leaving.

I tried drugs of all kinds and gave lip service to the thought of humility being something I didn't possess. I was a waste of time and space by most accounts, despite my best efforts to appear worthy of attention and desirable for love. I played a part in the play of life where I no longer knew what the costume was or if the part was still active. Only to be reminded every time I hit another wall constructed by my own hands and efforts, that I wasn't a good actor. And that maybe the play had been cancelled already.

I had more reasons than most to have shame and guilt remain mainstays in my perception of who I was. My lack of integrity to acknowledge such dispositions and do anything within my power to alleviate such emotional states and feelings propelled me further into despair. The repeating cycle of shame and guilt perpetuated more shame and guilt. I didn't even have the ability to see that shame and guilt are shared amongst all people at one time or another. An easier way to say that is I never lived in the land of shame and guilt, I only visited regularly. If you find yourself in an energy field of shame and guilt, life is done. You are reaching expiration. If what you are is shame and guilt. Or apathy or any of these lesser "realities" of existence, you are closer to the grave than you realize. Time is running out. You also open yourself up to possession and a lot of less than desirable things. Fortunately, most people do not live in a world of shame and guilt. They may experience it, but they don't live in it.

Self-pity is a favorite companion of shame and guilt. Followed by a quick targeted anger and judgment not only at the world, but also at God for giving you such a bad lot in life. "How could you be a loving God and allow this to happen to me?" I was spoiled and felt entitled to a life I had no part in helping to create. Mostly I wanted happiness despite not meeting God halfway or changing any of my destructive habits.

Shame and guilt are both destructive in nature, with each one representing different lower value points for self-judgment and self-esteem. Neither shame nor guilt do anything for the experiencer other than create more resentment toward humankind and life in general, and/or provide more ammunition for the story you tell yourself about how cruel God was to allow such horrible feelings to be present.

My experience with shame and guilt are probably not much different from most of you reading this. Neither of these words carried a positive connotation as I traveled through them. However, once I moved past believing I was these two aspects of a non-integrous life, I look back on both as necessary operations of the ego from which miracles could take place. When I speak of these two terms, I do not come from a place where my daily experience was racked by shame and guilt as a constant, but more from a place where I lived with these realities in spurts, usually based on past decisions which no longer represented who I was in the moment. Shame and guilt are tricky feelings. They appear justified at first glance, and few people investigate long enough to see what is actually being presented to them is only a partial reflection framed to appear a certain way. I ran away from these sensations the moment they arrived. And if I wasn't able to change my immediate mind about why I shouldn't feel a certain way, there was always alcohol to help. For me, alcohol became medicine. Alcohol, along with other drugs creates a barrier to the ego from being able to work against the host. At least for a little while. In essence, the effects that drinking heavy amounts of alcohol had on my consciousness was instant liberation from having to feel bad about myself in the moment. The part about alcohol that only the alcoholic realizes, and often times too late, is that alcohol might deliver you from feelings in the short term, but quickly delivers you back to yourself, without the aid of proper dopamine and serotonin levels, which the alcohol depletes, and without the aid of a clear mind when shame and guilt come visiting again. Alcohol was pals with my ego and they both knew the interchangeable roles they played. You, most likely do not have alcoholism as a barrier to transcending the ego. But quite possibly your barrier is right there with shame and guilt, and without stopping to feel these things then properly surrendering them over to a power greater than yourself, shame and guilt are here to stay, no matter how many miles you find yourself running in the interim, or how many self-help best sellers you read that aren't based on wisdom at all, just re-contextualized jargon made new again by a fresh perspective on the current society.

AA worked for me (Let me make it clear, I don't speak on behalf of the program of Alcoholics Anonymous) because I was battling alcoholism before I knew anything about the ego and was desperately looking for a way to stop drinking. If you're an alcoholic, you should put this book down and go check out a meeting. Do not use this work as a substitute for experiencing AA for yourself. AA is a total program of recovery, and what you have here is a story of experiencing God and freedom from the ego through the aid of the 12-steps, which are similar things at a particular level, but nowhere similar with concern to an active addiction to a substance.

Shame and guilt as a continual way of life bring almost certain death, imprisonment, suicide, and any other form of negative life experience associated with living at the bottom of the barrel. Shame and guilt can be a way of life, and believe it or not, these two areas of non-refuge are occupied as reality by millions of the world's population at the time I am writing this paragraph. And even while you are reading it.

To provide a little more info into what life looks like for someone operating at this level, we can reference back to Hawkins' Map of Consciousness and see that their view of God hovers somewhere between despising and vindictive. The general life-view for someone characterized by shame and guilt would be visibly witnessed as miserable and potentially evil, and these folks would quite literally cause the average person to walk the other way. The constant stream of emotions running, and unbeknownst to them ruining their life on a minute-to-minute basis are ones of blame and humiliation, and the folks unlucky enough to be residing in states of shame and/or guilt have two main courses of action for all those who find themselves in their path: destruction and/or elimination. Misery loves company is an apt saying for this level of calibration.

Circling back, what can be referred to as demonic

possession can occur when someone inhabits the levels of shame and guilt for long periods of time. It is not as if these levels create the possession, it is more that these levels help foster an attitude that creates a higher likelihood to be possessed by energy of lesser astral entities. Or more simply put, where you reside is what's around you. Currently, whether you acknowledge other realms as a possibility or not, they exist, and they exist ad infinitum. There are more parallel dimensions than all the grains of sand on all the beaches of our planet. Multiply that unknown number by infinity and you will have a basic understanding for how many parallel dimensions, astral planes, current lifetimes, etc. there are happening at this very moment. We experience life most of the time in this earth realm at this time and from a single vantage point. I classify it this way because I am not an expert on parallel dimensions and planes of existence, but trust me, there's a lot happening in other places than what we experience as right here and right now.

Our Earth plane is smack-dab in the middle of all the infinite possibilities for existence, and there are an infinite number of realms and dimensions emanating forth from us. As well as projecting backwards from us. As well as outwards in all directions simultaneously. Rules of infinity dictate that wherever you are is the center of everything, because you can never be at the beginning or end of infinity. Infinity doesn't have beginnings or ends.

Because of the nature of infinity, no matter where one finds oneself, they are always at the center of the evolutionary unfoldment of creation. Our particular realm is characterized by having a multitude of dimensions and opportunities for our soul's karmic evolutionary process. Every aspect of consciousness is a distinct and experienceable dimension. The only difference between someone experiencing heaven and someone experiencing hell is the dimension of consciousness they are inhabiting.

Our Earth realm allows us a full plethora of heaven and hell and everything in between. Other realms not so lucky as ours, don't have this. Other realms start at a calibrated level of enlightenment for every inhabitant coming into existence there. Heavenly realms exist inside and outside of our space time, and hellish realms exist in the same manner. However, both exist here and now as degrees of perception and interaction with the world.

As part of my experience with a level of consciousness that has taken on a life of its own in growth-rate and potential, regularly I am aware of dimensions operating with different parameters than ours. I can tell you something with certainty, and although my physical body did not live this lifetime within a prolonged experience of these energy levels, I have visited these realms characterized predominantly with shame and guilt. It is not a fun place to find oneself. There you find existence similar to ours, but total chaos at the same time. There is no mention of God, but there is still an inkling of possibility. These realms are reserved for those who choose an anti-God position, and therefore have the consequence of spending time in a hellish realm before heaven again becomes known. God is always but a choice away. So, if you ever find yourself stuck in one of these levels of consciousness or in one of these realms through astral projection or other means of exploration, do yourself a favor and cry out to God. Only the energies of immense Love can save you from hell. Don't believe anything otherwise. Or risk an eternity spent trying to figure out the very thing that was just shared here freely.

I tell you all of this not to scare you, or to make it seem like I live in the land of the "woo woo's," but I tell you all of this because there is much more beyond what is seen and unseen, and at a certain point you will find yourself down in the dumps, possibly depressed, and possibly clinically depressed, and it is at those times you will need to remember what you read here. Typically, within bouts of depression, one will endure prolonged experiences of shame and guilt, but fear not, for the tools you will learn here will serve you well if you ever find your life consumed by such low attracter fields. When one transcends the states of shame and guilt, they have in turn transcended aspects of and attachments to the ego, but in no way the entirety of the personal ego.

Now that we have a slightly better understanding of shame and guilt from a consciousness and non-linear perspective, let's dive back into the physical realm and take a look at how dictionary.com defines the terms in question:

Shame: *The painful feeling arising from the consciousness of something dishonorable, improper, ridiculous, etc., done by oneself or another*

Guilt: *a feeling of responsibility or remorse for some offense, crime, wrong, etc., whether real or imagined.*

These definitions are at the heart of what most people experience as defined models of shame and guilt. For the average person, they will not live in the world of constant shaming and incessant guilt but will only visit these realities from time to time as the ego sees fit to engage their thought process.

One of the most astonishing bits of knowingness that came during my upswing in consciousness, which came around the time I crossed into the level of love, was that our thoughts fuel our feelings, and our feelings fuel our emotions. And if we want to change how we feel about a thing we must first change how we witness our thoughts. Emotions are comprised of many feelings, and feelings are comprised of thousands of habitual thought patterns, and thought patterns are the byproduct of what one allows into their brain, mixed with how the ego chooses to manifest that allowed stimuli into the day-to-day psyche of the average human experience. Quite literally, our experience with the world is the byproduct of nature and nurture, and the old adage of "garbage in, garbage out" holds specifically true in the world of thinkingness. We will spend more time breaking this contextual understanding down as the book progresses, but for now all that is needed to move into the next part of this chapter is understanding a simple truth: what we hold in mind tends to manifest.

In the next section in this chapter, we will look at what four different enlightened masters had to say with regards to the nature of life, and not only what they had to say about a particular topic, but the similarity between each master's teaching portrayed in religious texts, which served as a major blessing for me when going through my evolution of consciousness. Once you read through the quotes from Christianity, Buddhism, Hinduism, and Daoism, there will be a short thought detailing with how shame and guilt can be re-contextualized to better serve the understanding for transcending the ego as the basis for Step One of this program.

TRUTHS:

(The Gospel of Luke) *The kingdom of God is not coming in any way that you can observe. The kingdom of God is already here - within you.*

(The Dhammapada) *Those with a pure heart, and who seek the Way* *without ceasing, will find it. It is like cleaning glass until the dust is removed.*

(The Bhagavad Gita) *Those who seek to find the One without ceasing, will find the Lord dwelling in their own hearts.*

(The Tao Te Ching) *In bygone days men of wisdom honored the Way by declaring that it could be found by all who seek it.*

CONTEMPLATING ON TRUTH:

I spent more than thirty-two years searching high and low for the kingdom of God. More accurately, I spent that amount of time searching for a connection to the God of my ancestors' understanding, while unknowingly doing my best to create a separation from the Creator through my conscious decisions and actions, and through my sub-conscious programming related to guilt and personal feelings about myself and the world around me. It was not until I was thirty-three that I experientially knew that God, the Creator of the Universe, the Sustainer of the Cosmos, the Magnificent and Ultimate Authority of life and death, was not to be found anywhere outside of me, but had been with me and within me the entire time. Not outside but inside I found God. Right there within my being was the connection I searched for. Within myself was the connection to the divine. God was not coming in any way I could observe externally, but rather, God was moving towards me in the still and small space of my quieted being, communicating through a voiceless and loving whisper, "Welcome back, I'm glad you found me. Now what, my son?"

You see, God isn't over there doing things with other people in other far-away places. God is right here, right now, with you all the time, because you and God are not in fact separate, you're one. Only you can't see that yet. And if you can't see what's directly in front of you, why hold onto outdated feelings and programs of shame and guilt any longer? Shame and guilt do two things well. First, they convince people they're real. Second, they make a person believe God is that which punishes you. You're your own judge, you're your own tormenter. God isn't found in your torment. God doesn't take pride and joy in your suffering or self-indulgences, because experiencing God isn't found in shame or guilt, but rather in love and forgiveness. Love and forgiveness aren't found out there. They're found within. Because of this, love and forgiveness not only bless the world around you, but within you simultaneously. One can't change the world around them before acknowledging how the world is but a reflection of what's happening inside of them. If you seek happiness, choose love and forgiveness in every moment as opposed to fear and judgment, for it is loving yourself that creates happiness and healing and love in the world around you. The inside-first approach is the only approach that works if you desire true happiness and endless joy.

Life has a funny way of showing a person their truest potential as a human being. It does not wait around for one to manifest it, but more allows room and growth to realize it. It is solely upon when I or another are ready to accept a view of life through another lens. Every moment contains an opportunity to present that. This book from one lens is a love letter to the gift of choice. For many years, I put everything of the world in front of simply being. Namely, addictions, the quest for power, the desire for physical intimacy, the wanting of security, the hope for riches and the trappings of an ego-inspired life. My personal ego needed to be cleansed and the mind needed to be dusted off through the process of surrender before I was able to see my truest potential – the potential that is within all who pursue life with a pure heart while choosing to move towards a transcended mind, which is waiting for all who seek God without ceasing while consistently surrendering the lesser for the greater, the just-around-the-corner expressions of the ego for the certain but prolonged future of realized potential. Fear is the motivation of the ego, and it was fear which dominated my intentions both consciously and sub-consciously before learning the obvious but seemingly at times hidden secret of "cleaning one's glass until the dust is removed." You see, one does not clean one's own glass. In fact, you can't. You can only notice the dust and ask God to clean it for you. In life, we have but a small number of actual choices, and all choices boil down to a single series at a certain point: noticing dirt in our vision or looking past it through muddled lenses, and then choosing more ignorance or, although uncertain-where-it-leads, surrender.

The path to healing, happiness, joy and even enlightenment begins for those who allow the guilt and shame dust on the glass in front of them to be washed away by the hands of their creator, through the process of surrendering the lesser fear-based experiences of the ego for the greater loving-truths found beyond one's mind. The mind is but an instrument for the human experience, and it is far from the greatest aspect of being a human. The mind plays a part in this game of life by allowing programs to appear as if real, but once one surrenders over the programs of the mind, the promise of what's found beyond mind becomes evident, and one now has the opportunity for actual happiness and continual joy as a reality. Shame and guilt reside in the mind, but not in what comes once one transcends the ego.

Shame and guilt can either be seen as the messengers from Life that can direct one's way upward towards enlightenment and a conscious connection with the divine, or as the tools needed to help dig an emotional grave in preparation for an eventual physical death. The shame I felt over addictions, and the guilt I carried for allowing my life to sink to such a level of depravity were two realities that kept me stuck in the rat race of self-pity and despair, with both serving as amplifiers of a victimhood mentality. I let shame and guilt run my life for a period of time, with the byproduct being the arrival at a moment where I needed to make the choice to either live a different way or continue dying emotionally until I physically arrived at death's doorstep.

Thankfully, I chose to surrender my life and will over to a power greater than myself and began again to seek the nameless and voiceless One. Over a relatively short period of time, my personal vantage point went from a constant experience of self-pity to a regular connection and experience of self-love, and all because once I surrendered my hopeless state for an unknown one, on the other side I found the One had never left myside. God, the One, the Creator/Sustainer, Allah, Yahweh or whatever name given to deity that fits the mold you align with, that power is not just found in other parts of the world and universe, it's residing within you as well as all around you. God is everywhere all the time and nowhere in particular, so when you call out for help and meet that call with action and different decision making, God has a way of helping those who help themselves to more of God. We have the choice to choose a different path at any part of this journey. No amount of will without God, however, is enough to choose anew and experience the peace that heading north creates. We can choose anew, but it's actually a power greater than our self that gives us the context of choice to begin with. Because God is context and content, we're never separated. So, when you surrender your shame and guilt (which are pieces of content) over to God, that step starts developing a recontextualization of life, a reorientation of life, and a resurgence of possibility in your life to contextualize and manifest love present with every step you take moving forward.

With the removal of shame and guilt from my inner being through the act of surrendering them to a power greater than myself, I was free to move upwards on the path to prolonged happiness, increased joy, and at the time, the hope of enlightenment in this lifetime. I was not alone in my search for a better Life, and I was not alone in my desire to connect with the divine. And from the ledge of continued serenity I now lie perched, I can honestly say, the Way can be found and honored by all those who seek it, not just by the blessed men of antiquity and supposed wisdom from a bygone age, but by you reading these words now.

The first two stumbling blocks to living the life I always hoped was possible were taken away from the terrain below my feet when surrender became the last option before death, and with that act came the immediate understanding and eventual knowingness that the same miracle is possible for anyone else who has the courage to acknowledge their own bouts with these two negative forces, realizes for their own self that they no longer wish to be slave to the ego and the manifestations of shame and guilt, and makes the choice to move towards the Way without ceasing. Transcending guilt and shame means one is no longer under the impression they are what they feel when moments of shame and guilt creep in, but instead understand that to feel these things are moments of teaching happening "for us" to grow and to learn and not "to us" as punishment for past sins.

Surrender is the key to growth and seeking the Way, and without surrender, you'll find that moving past the confines of the mind will be impossible, let alone achievable through modern medicine or personal willpower. At this point it must be stated, there is no joy without truth, and it is truth the Way proposes. The truth is sometimes seen in everyday life amongst peers and bedfellows, but always within the still and quiet moments of those brave enough to admit to God that humility is worth embracing. That's where it grows. Those who humble themselves with surrender are the same who will inherit heaven here on earth, and conversely, those who choose the world over the Way, will find life repeating in a circular motion in not just this lifetime, but in the next as well. From experience, walking the straight and narrow path is easier than going in circles. And more rewarding as well.

INSTRUCTIONS FOR STEP ONE:

Find a quiet space away from the noise of other people and from the busyness of the world. If you find yourself making it to this step and you cannot escape what's around you and you're ready to take this step, don't worry about where you are, just close your eyes for a moment or two and take a few deep breaths to begin. This step can be taken by speaking the words below internally or externally, but I would recommend doing both in succession and then writing them down after you're finished reciting them. What this step means, is that you realize the impact the mind plays on your daily life, and the way it presents thoughts, feelings and emotions which are rarely asked for or chosen. By taking this step, you are choosing humility in the form of surrender of that which you cannot control, the ego/mind, and starting to let go of your attachment to the belief that you are what you think, feel and emote. The magic of this step is the recontextualization it provides the experiencer once admitting to one's self and the world around you that yes, in fact, I have no control over this thing called mind and its goings-on. By taking this step, you are informing God, I am ready to see what life has in store for me no longer being unwarily attached to my personal ego, and no longer remaining attached to the belief system that I am anything other than a child of God, infinite in nature, and because of these facts, I am ready to chase after truth within the pathway provided here and found as a by-product of working the 12 steps.

STEP ONE

-

I admit I am powerless over my ego, and my life up until this point has been managed and run by it, but I am ready to find truth despite not knowing it personally yet.

STEP ONE PRAYER

-

I surrender over my ego to Thee oh Lord, in its entirety, and all attachments I have to the belief that I am my mind. Thank you for how this decision will impact my life positively from this point forward.

Chapter 2

TRANSCENDING THE FORCES OF APATHY & GRIEF

Believing in a Power greater than myself was the key...

Dictionary.com defines apathy as *"absence or suppression of passion, emotion, or excitement."* But with regards to apathy in the spiritual sense, it is much more insidious than that. Dictionary.com defines grief as *"keen mental suffering or distress over affliction or loss, sharp sorrow; painful regret."* As with the case of apathy, grief from a spiritual sense has a darker connotation. As manifestations of the ego, both apathy and grief as current states of consciousness are far more detrimental and can be described as end-of-the road expressions of life for the individual. That's so much more than mere absence of passion or keen mental suffering.

There were two times in my life when I had direct experience with prolonged visitation of these negative forces. One was as a child when my father passed away, and the second was as an adult when my alcoholism was in full swing. Both times, I was at low points characterized by what we'll dive into deeper, but suffice it to say, not only were these energies present within me, but transcendence over them took place as well. No matter how low we feel, or how dejected we become, or how much we blame God for our current state of affairs, or how sad our life is, God is always present and waiting for us to cry out for help in a sincere way. God does not deny God when help is needed. God does not get angry with us for making less than stellar choices. God is not a human in the sense that anger and judgment are part of God's make-up. Those are human foibles. There are many who would have us believe God takes joy in people's misery and sadness and looks to judge us because of it. This couldn't be further from the truth. God does not judge us; we judge ourselves. What we are is the only judgment necessary, and the only way to be lifted from deep seated judgments about ourselves and their corresponding prison walls created by such, is to humbly and sincerely ask God to help remove these walls and set us squarely back at even, so moving towards truth is a possibility in this lifetime.

The levels of grief and apathy are not to be played with, because within these two levels one comes face to face with the doorway to almost the point of no return. Grief and apathy as sidebars to regular life usually take on the characteristics of temporal feelings related to "I wish I had done more," or "of course I messed up, I always do, why should I even try," or "things never work out for me," and my personal favorite, "the world is out to get me."

I bring up these particular expressions of grief and mentation's of apathy because I have also experienced the same sentimentalities at various points along life's journey. Regardless of briefly experiencing such depressing states of awareness, or regularly finding yourself stuck in the muck of both expressions of the fear spectrum, these two illusions are levels of consciousness that are not to be taken lightly once they arise. The transcendent gift of surrender must be applied immediately to the moments when apathy and grief first become known and arise and when they present themselves. It doesn't matter if they're just visiting or starting to unpack their bags, these two forces always arrive heavy and daunting.

Grief and apathy have particular juices innate within them for the host ego which attract similar energies when these thoughts or feeling states are allowed to be indulged in, or allowed to fully transform into an emotional state of being. Recognizing our choice of indulgence and our intent to remain indulging are the keys to understanding their ability to rapidly build momentum into realities capable of what can feel like a never-ending loop of misery. The keyword "juice" in the sentence above, is an important one to understand and eventually know as part of your Spidey senses. I did not come up with this term "juiced." I most commonly have heard David R. Hawkins refer to the word as a means of describing the payoff a person's ego gets when they indulge in the particular style of self-pity that grief and apathy falsely present, as well as what other lower attracter fields certainly allow for. What I learned early on through Hawkins's teaching is that the lower attracter fields in and of themselves do not have the power required to keep someone stuck in the muck, but the juice that they provide for self-ridicule and personal condemnation is the lynchpin in understanding their effectiveness when used by the ego to destroy an otherwise lovely day. The forces of apathy and grief are not what keep the individual stuck in agony, it's the actual continuing to choose the juice they provide the person as what's self-destructive, which almost forces the host to stay within a comfort zone not comfortable to most.

The personal ego thrives when it finds a comfort zone for the host in a place of discomfort. It then builds its foundation there with a repetitive cycle of the host believing they are the feelings, thoughts and emotions that come from such a detrimental foundation of this "uncomfortable comfort zone." There's a lie we tell ourselves consistently. When I was drinking I would be filled with grief over making poor choices. I would then drink to subdue the grief. And then would find myself back again at a state of apathy because I got drunk to hide the grief. I was then incapable of doing anything. So I would repeat the process.

These negative states result in a repetition but it's the repetition of choosing to continually indulge in this that keeps the cycle going. And the secret to breaking the cycle is not choosing to indulge in it. But when in it, we don't have the willpower to not choose the belief system that we are anything but this cycle. This is why the moment we sense the presence of apathy and grief we have to surrender them over immediately. We don't want to get into that cycle. No one finds God in that cycle. As a sidebar, this is how people stay stuck in hell. When we believe we are the cycle, when we believe we are grief and apathy, we are unable to see ourselves as anything else. When we allow the cycle to cement itself as reality, then God becomes judgment and condemnation. As stated, in reality, God does not judge us. We judge ourselves. And the "we" that judges ourselves is the ego, the god we believe ourselves to be.

We hold onto outdated stories about who and what we are. We like how it makes us feel to hold onto these things, regardless of their destruction while we are indulging ourselves in the memory or the wake those memories leave behind once gone. We're addicted to the juice of being angry. We're addicted to the juice of being sad. We're addicted to the juice of being the victim. We get to feel justified in our resentment of life if we have the continual juice needed to remain resentful. The reason people allow themselves to find comfort in what many would describe as uncomfortable, is because as long as they're the victim, they're somebody, and for the personal ego, being somebody is always better than being nobody.

Even being the king of sadness allows the ego to be king of something. The personal ego fears being seen as less than what's present, so it allows for states of depression and agony all in the name of survival. We feed off of the juice of things and the stories we tell ourselves about particular moments in time, not the actual moments in time. Moments are just moments, nothing more, nothing less. But stories can last forever.

The good news is that for the most part, those of you reading this are not or will not remain in the states of grief and apathy for serious lengths of time, unless otherwise prompted by the onset of serious depression or the sudden loss of someone dear to you. For the purpose of these two lower levels of consciousness, we will talk more about how to use them as motivators as opposed to that which brings continual stress.

The juice we get when we inhabit a particularly negative thought pattern, as with grief and apathy, can give someone an immediate sense of righteousness and moral superiority. This can be seen in the rebuttal by many afflicted with grief and apathy: "you just don't understand, bad stuff always happens to me and there is nothing I can do about it." Or any other version of this sentiment that fits your fancy. One of the favorite distractions the ego likes to use when keeping us separate from that which we really are, is keeping us separate from those around us who can help our situation through empathy of shared experiences. The personal ego not only wants us separate from higher and higher truths, but apart from love in any form when still playing victim.

When I was in the darkest of my drinking days I withdrew from society, and not because I chose to do so in a willing fashion, but because my ego told me time and time again that I wasn't good for anyone, I wasn't worth anything, and that all I could do to someone else was cause pain and misery. At first, when the ego tried this trick, I laughed it off as goofy thinking, but as the disease of alcoholism went into full swing, I began believing the thoughts, and then the belief became compounded by the juice I got from being right about no one wanting to hang around even though I was the one choosing to be around fewer and fewer people. The personal ego sets up isolation and manipulates truth through self-fulfilling prophesies. My reasoning for being alone turned inward and became solidified against reproach, and all because I started to get a rush at inhabiting the victim mentality. And always soon to follow in short order was a reaffirmation from my ego that I indeed had nothing to offer anyone, for there was no one in my life to offer it to.

My logic was skewed, and based out of a defeated sense of self-worth, brought on by years of allowing my ego to run wild. What was hard to see amongst the sea of fallen tears that covered my apartment far and wide, is that beneath it all, beneath the grief and apathy, beneath the juice I got from proving my isolationist theory correct time and time again, was the desire to approach life once more from a different angle. And thus, the cycle of grief over past mistakes and apathy over current circumstances would play out in fine fashion once more because at the time I was not powerful enough to overcome the repetition of negativity or humble enough to ask for help.

The cycle of being juiced by lower attracter fields and the cycle of maintaining lower levels of consciousness is nauseating at best, but it becomes the best you're familiar with. The ego wins a mighty battle when it becomes better for the human to isolate than to enjoy the warmth of the sunshine breaking its way through shut blinds.

The juice of the lower consciousness levels is what in part keeps people addicted to them, and while there is an active addiction, whether it be to drugs or alcohol, or to the ego's portrayal of life, it remains difficult to see the sunshine for what it is, without first asking God for help with opening those blinds. Apathy and grief are the gateway drugs to death, and they are the last two emotional sets which lead the individual into the lowest depths of hell while still in this body. The only cure for transcending the ego when these two forces of hell come calling is to see each illusion for what it is, an illusion, and surrender over the feelings and the juice associated with said feelings as soon as you possibly can. The only salvation possible to transcend prolonged visits to these desperate ways of living is through a higher power reaching down upon sincere request and removing someone from their current life predicament. When all else fails, God is the answer. Likewise, when all else works, God was the answer. And that is true whether the question was pondered on or not.

Another point worth discussing is willpower. I thought for the longest time willpower would deliver me from the bondage of self. But what I never knew because it is not common knowledge, and certainly was not brought to my attention at the time, willpower is only as strong as the level of consciousness you currently calibrate at. The world sees an addict or an alcoholic and says they just need more willpower. But what I know as truth now is that someone who is a slave to their ego and addictions, in no way shape or form has the willpower needed to overcome anything. The interesting thing is addictions and their corresponding levels of consciousness calibrate very low on Hawkins's Map of Consciousness. To illustrate, self-loathing, unlovable, riddled with fear, desperate for relief *me* calibrated extremely low. But one drink in after work – a drink that began with the equivalent of six shots of vodka before I added a splash of cranberry – and I became freed from the bondage of those feelings to experience temporary love and relief and a level of comfort vastly superior to where I was when I first started to pour that drink. I was subduing the fears associated with life in favor of something temporarily far greater, and that's why the alcoholic repeats the cycle. You go from hell to heaven in – what? – six minutes. Only to experience the grief once again. And the cycle starts all over. What you're searching for isn't to get drunk or to get high, but how you feel when you're drunk or high. The problem is you only get to visit those states when you are drunk or high. You don't actually live there.

It's important to know that while one person can help another person, no one person has the power to save another. It takes a power of something much greater than yourself or of anyone else you come in contact with to relieve your sufferings at times when they appear their darkest. Only God, and the power of love at an immense level can do the trick. God, however, sends people to help people. If you asked Mother Teresa how is it that you can help thousands of lepers, she would say, "I'm not doing anything." The love that someone is brings relief, not the physical person. Truth, which I use as synonymous with love throughout, is what brings lasting relief. Believing in your grief or apathy is far from knowing the truth. The direct image of someone's joy and happiness brings relief. As a quick aside, a person doesn't heal another person by their actions or beliefs, and a person does not perform miracles along the same vein. Healing and miracles arise from within the field which that person inhabits or calls upon to be present. If you see another seemingly healed from the presence of another person, it has nothing to do with the personage of the person who you think healed the individual, it has everything to do with what was allowed to come through that person to perform the miracle of healing without medicine.

So, on the day when I cried out to God for help with my

alcoholism, which I now know was merely my ego run wild manifesting itself in the form of addiction, it was God's power and love that saved me from the hell I was living in, and not my mother's worry, or my friend's advice, or my willpower that had anything to do with it.

When one reaches the bottom of whatever floorless foundation they call the absolute depths of depravity, only a power far greater than yourself can help you find your way out of the darkness. Knowing that now as an absolute is freeing to say the least, and it also happens to be where some of this 12–step magic starts to present itself. If you reread the sentence above again from a slightly different perspective, you might also catch that having God be the only source of one's deliverance from the dark into the light is what it takes to effortlessly let go of one's attachment to the juices of grief and apathy, because you were never in control of the energy of despair to begin with. They were just unruly visitors who outwore their welcome but continued to strongarm you for prolonged inhabitance.

The mere act of asking for help with an earnest desire to be better, along with doing the work you'll find within this book or among any 12-step group, is all it takes to be better and receive that help. It really is that simple. So do me, and yourself, a favor and don't try to overcomplicate it. The ego is the base root of overcomplicating things, and by now we should all agree that the ego is not our friend who helps us out in times of anguish, but the friend we all have that talks about us behind our back and who starts drama for the sake of feeling better about themselves.

As a last bit of information before moving onto hearing from the spiritual masters of ages past, we will look a little closer at what characteristics grief and apathy have as their basis for consciousness calibration through information provided by Dr. Hawkins. Not only for the person inhabiting the lower consciousness levels of apathy and grief, but also the average man or woman who finds themselves visiting the land of apathy and grief. Each will find these characteristics particularly familiar: their basic view of God fluctuates between disdainful at best and condemning at worst, which means the ego has the opportunity at these lower levels to do serious damage to an otherwise already compromised state of being in the world. The life-view of someone within these levels of consciousness is slightly better than someone operating from a place of shame and guilt, but only because evil has not yet completely overtaken their psyche; tragic and hopeless are the main ways someone sees their life when coming from apathy or grief, to the degree that any attempt at making life better is defeated before ever trying. The emotions most commonly associated with these levels of the ego's dominance are based in regret and despair, and without the help of a higher power to rescue someone from these depths of self-loathing, time is running out for hope to ever be present again. The last aspects of grief and despair worth noting are the processes with which someone coming from these attracter fields manages to work throughout their daily lives, with despondency and abdication being the dominant overarching catalysts for progress.

Being able to see these levels from an objective standpoint brings about the understanding needed to embrace the knowledge that the ego does not have our best interests at heart. At one point the ego may seem like a well-rounded travel companion, but it is at the levels of grief and apathy that the human being is at the cliffs of almost total destruction. Despondency means to lose all hope or courage, and the byproduct of losing all hope or courage is a very low sense of self-worth, and an almost nonexistent sense of worthiness in general. Abdication is a step further down the rung of fortune, and basically means that the person coming from a state of apathy, or even just visiting it for a short while, is likely to not only have no self-worth left, but begins bartering with the devil as it were, for the chance of even a morsel of serenity. The ego would rather sell your soul and allow you to give up all your rights as a child of God, than see you succeed past its grasp in any way. At the level of grief, the ego still holds on to hope that its best days are ahead, but once someone reaches the doorway of apathy and decides to walk willingly into its clutches, even the ego starts to jump ship and leave you almost altogether, and subsequently relinquishes its vessel to the lowest levels of luciferic manipulation. The reason demonic possession can start occurring at this level is because not even the mind and logic is left to reason against it.

Now is a good time to talk a little bit about luciferic energy, how it uses temptation, and how the luciferic manifests itself no matter how close to God one grows. Have no fear though, for the luciferic does not actually represent an entity in and of itself worthy of fear, but more or less represents the energy of that which is almost completely cut off from the sunlight of redemption. I would be hiding the truth from you if I didn't let you know that there is in fact an entity named lucifer, and that the energy this entity represents has byproducts that can manifest as demonic and satanic. The reality of this entity, however, is not that it is an equal field general to Jesus, or able to bring about the end times, but that it is a pesky sideshow not worth entertaining. I have come into contact with this entity several times since surrendering my life over to God, and in each encounter the result has been the same: awareness of the presence and then casting the presence out with either a command to leave in the name of Jesus, or by invoking the power and love of God the creator. Lucifer is not worth your time, energy, or any amount of worry, for even the smallest amount of love is volumes greater than the best attempt that this luciferic energy represents.

In the lowest levels of consciousness, as found in apathy, guilt, and then shame, the demonic energies begin to not only create a life very few would wish on their most despised of enemies, but the energy itself creates a gateway for lower astral entities having the opportunity to inhabit the human being. These entities are comprised of lower astral beings and what the world would call demons, who either have not crossed into the next phase, or they represent energies that manifest from parallel lives within parallel dimensions. Once someone calibrates at levels above these forces, they no longer have the threat of these entities becoming pronounced within them. And once a calibrated level of courage or higher is reached, this energy comes only in the forms of temptations and ego-driven thought patterns.

What I just said may sound like hocus pocus, but trust me, it's not energy you want to play with or have the unfortunate opportunity to come in contact with while calibrating at these lower levels yourself. For the time being, the only advice worth giving is that when you find yourself flirting with prolonged experiences of grief and apathy, your only hope for being saved is to cry out to the Creator for rescue. And mean it with every fiber of your being.

Many of you reading this book will have either heard about or taken part in astral projection for yourself, or you will become interested in it as a past-time at some point in your life. Or perhaps many of you will not, but nevertheless, the realms filled with these lower astral energies will present themselves to you as a possible location for your wandering spirit to travel to at one point or another in your evolution of consciousness. I would advise not vacationing there or booking any travel to these realms, no matter how curious you are to see what this kind of life is all about.

This next part of the chapter is my favorite aspect of this book. It is because we get to here from four teachers of the highest ilk who walked the earth before us. As I have stated earlier, but will rephrase slightly here, whether you consider yourself a Christian, a Buddhist, Hindu or Daoist, your religious figurehead often holds more wisdom in an attributed sentence than all of the new age gurus combined, and it is because of this that I am glad God chose their words to be included in this book.

TRUTHS:

(The Dhammapada) *Seeking within, you will find stillness. Here there is no more fear or attachment - only joy.*

(The Bhagavad Gita) *Those who find the Way are those who have love and forgiveness in their hearts.*

(The Tao Te Ching) *The Way is mighty, yet people prefer smaller paths.*

(The Gospel of John) *I am a beacon of light to those who see me. I am a mirror to those who look for me. I am a door to those who knock on me. I am a Way for you, the traveler.*

CONTEMPLATING ON TRUTH:

No matter what I searched for out in the world I was perpetually left wanting more and feeling increasingly inadequate at what I found, leaving me always only wanting more. The problem with looking outside of one's self with the hope of "getting fixed," is that it brings about further attachments to the impermanence of life, and those attachments bring with them the fears that one is not enough currently (grief), nor will one be enough in the future (apathy). Looking within, past what I thought myself to be, past the confines of the personal ego, and past the landscape of the mind, all for answers and for fulfillment did just the opposite to searching in the world. It gave real hope and lasting momentum free of fear or attachment to what I found. Whether I thought a nicer car would make me feel more accomplished, or a bigger house would create more security, or physical intimacy from a stranger would make me feel more loved, or the flashy sparkle of jewelry would make me feel above someone else, or a deep-dive into the false teachings of our modern day, social media, snake oil salesmen, aka "guru-based-influencers," would make me feel momentarily enlightened by their reused wisdom – none of it lasted or created a connection with the divine worth repeating.

The outside world has a way of making people think what we're searching for can be found somewhere outside of us, but in all reality, what we're searching for is found within and beneath the stillness of our being. We don't experience Love through the content of life, but it's the context from which that content arises where Love is found. If one spends their life looking for more and more things to make them happy, they'll spend their entire life disappointed and angry. Attachments and expectations are the root of suffering. When one expects to find lasting happiness in a new relationship, or in a new car, or new promotion, or new whatever, attachment to this expectation and its results soon follow. "I thought this or that was supposed to make me happy!" But after getting this or that, wanting soon starts up again. Lasting happiness and joy are found within – they are not found out there amongst the billboards promoting more "wantingness" and further attachments.

More so today than in years past, personally, the words "love" and "forgiveness" appear as actions as opposed to pretty thoughts. Consequently, when I currently meditate on what "heart" means, it no longer solely means my predisposition towards others and myself based on how I feel about them or me, but how I choose to act towards the collective "we" in word and deed. So in actuality, in this context, the word "heart" can be seen as an action word as well. We have all heard the term "they're all heart," and if someone you know is "all heart" it is because that person displays acts of love and forgiveness in their daily life. We are defined by others mostly based upon our actions, and if I desire to be defined not by past decisions but by future acts, what better way to start redefining myself than with the actions of love and forgiveness, as opposed to ones inspired by grief and apathy? The purification of my heart starts with love and forgiveness for myself, followed by love and forgiveness for the world around me. Then loving and forgiving acts towards others on a moment-to-moment basis.

Love and forgiveness are the action steps of the heart, and they are also the steps necessary to find the Way, in solitude or out amongst the wolves. Heart, as it's described in spiritual literature, is not an organ found within the body, but more akin to decision making, namely, putting someone else's needs above your own, or at least on an even playing field. "Coming from the heart," is another way of saying, "I recognize you as equal to me, and because of this fact, I have gratitude for you and your story." Coming from the heart by practicing love and forgiveness is one way to God, and it's a viable understanding of the tenets of Christianity. Jesus came forth from the heart of God, as Love manifested, for the hearts of man, to be a guidepost for all who seek to know what love and forgiveness look like lived out. Krishna, as expounded on within the Bhagavad Gita, is quoted above as giving one all the information they need to find God, or as he describes it, "The Way," through the quote above: "Those who find the Way are those who have love and forgiveness in their hearts." Love and forgiveness are not always easy to practice, mostly because people often feel unloved and not forgiven in their own life. However, the trick to finding God in one's daily life is to first start by forgiving yourself and forgiving God. Then love has a chance to start growing in pastures ready for an eventual harvest capable of feeding many.

Throughout life, I can mark the years and days gone-by with preferences for choosing smaller paths than what I do now.

Through loveless sex and revolving partners, I chose a smaller path.

Through self-imposed misery and inevitable self-defeat, I chose a smaller path.

Through uninvestigated anger directed outwards at others and the world around me, I chose a smaller path.

Through complaining about life and distancing myself from the Way, I chose a smaller path.

Through embracing pride as a viable means of self-expression, and through choosing both envy and jealousy as important means to an end, I chose a smaller path.

Through holding onto grief and apathy as unshakable comforts, I chose a smaller path.

Through abusing drugs and alcohol as an escape from life, I chose a smaller path.

Through limiting God in my everyday life, I chose a smaller path.

Through fear of the future, I chose a smaller path.

Through regret of the past, I chose a smaller path.

Through worry about how people thought of me, I chose a smaller path.

Through selfishness and dishonesty, I chose a smaller path.

Today, however, I mark my days and moments not by choosing smaller paths, but by conscious decisions directed towards experiencing the Mighty Way. Today, my head holds high and my shoulders rear back as I fearlessly move from perfect moment to perfect moment – for today, I choose not the smaller path but the road less traveled, the road of union with the divine – the life of a humbled servant and not and emboldened slave. People choose smaller paths for various reasons: either they haven't heard about another way of going about life, or they don't know how to go about living life another way. Or they're scared to pursue another way of life due to current comforts or laziness in their present routine for sameness with the masses. When one chooses the Mighty Way, they're choosing uncertainty and faith in something unseen and unknown yet. But for those who have made the choice to chase after God, and found God, all report back that the Way is Mighty indeed. So, as you look around your life, as you sit back and ponder on the greatest adventure a person could embark upon in this lifetime, what's more intriguing than finding out if God is real or not? And simultaneously finding out what happens once you have had a direct experience with such immense truth?

If one seeks to know God in this life and not just understand what other people proclaim about divinity, it helps to meet godly men and women along the way, in order to help keep one focused on the end goal of reaching max potential as a spiritual being. In our darkest hours we all need someone or something to guide us towards the light. We all need a mirror to show us what we are and what we are not. And while traveling our chosen path, doesn't it make the journey more enjoyable to know we have a companion? A companion to help us keep our current pace?

I believe Jesus is not saying that through only his likeness you will find needed forgiveness, but instead, by following his actions we all have a chance to find The Way for ourselves, or to see Truth in our own life, and to experience Light on our journey towards completeness and reconnection and lived forgiveness. And if it's not Jesus one reaches for in their darkest and most light-filled times, then maybe it's Krishna, or the Buddha, or another enlightened being not quite on the level of a living Avatar.

Jesus, for me, was what I was brought up loving as a child and early adult. Jesus, for me, was the goal and the hopeful destination. I hold none above Jesus. But I've come to realize knowing is always more powerful than understanding. So today, I place none above Jesus in stature, but I also know there are some who can call themselves brothers and sisters with the divine. I know today, that learning from Jesus and living out the pathway of service and surrender, one too has the chance at a certain point in this lifetime or the next, to call Jesus both Love, Savior and Brother in the same breath. Seeing others as God sees them, starts with but a simple choice: choose to follow someone who's light shines bright enough to light your path. Once you're in unison with light, your entire village gets an opportunity to see through the darkness. At this point, you'll realize that religion doesn't lead to God, but that it's only a part of understanding which leads to knowingness.

INSTRUCTIONS FOR STEP TWO:

Find a quiet space away from the noise of other people and from the busyness of the world. If you find yourself making it to this step and you cannot escape what's around you and you're ready to take this step, don't worry about where you are, just close your eyes for a moment or two and take a few deep breaths. This step can be taken by speaking the words below internally or externally, but I would recommend doing both in succession and then writing them down after you're finished reciting them. What this step means, is that you recognize that without the aid of something greater than yourself it is not possible to transcend your attachments to the ego/mind and the world around you. And that by staying in the place where the mind is what you believe you are, you are missing out on the opportunity to move past mind and into a world where love is more abundant and happiness is known and not just understood.

The power of this step is also found within in the humility to admit that you are not powerful enough to do this act on your own. If you were you would not be here taking this step. This step has truth within it to the degree with which you profess honestly a choice to surrender over the notion that you have the power needed for helping yourself, in exchange for power coming from something greater than you, regardless if you believe in something greater than you or not.

By taking this step, you are reaffirming that faith is a choice you're making, and it's not faith in the author of this work, but faith in the redeeming power of that which created you. Or that which you cannot define but hope exists. You do not need to believe in God to take this step, or even use the word God, but you do have to choose humility in the face of doubt about divinity and come from a place of admitting you don't know the truth about divinity. You cannot trick divinity into believing you, so it's paramount that honesty is your guiding principle. The key to surrender is radical honesty.

STEP TWO

-

I have come to believe that a power greater than myself can remove the blocks to transcending my ego, and in and of myself, I do not have the power to do so.

STEP TWO PRAYER

-

I let go of that which binds me, that which I have attachments to, and that which I have set expectations on. Thank you, Lord, for hearing this prayer, and for loving me more than I love myself.

Chapter 3

TRANSCENDING THE FORCES
OF FEAR & DESIRE

It was time to choose Life...

If you haven't been able to tell yet, throughout this book the main way that a spiritual aspirant or just a common civilian transcends the forces of fear and the attachment to their ego is through surrender. Surrender is always the first step in reaching heights of truth that are not just understood but become part of one's knowingness. Surrender is the key to unlocking one "ah-ha" moment after another "ah-ha" moment, which as we talked about earlier, serves to recontextualize your life every time a higher truth comes in and replaces an old paradigm of understanding.

The first section of the book is dedicated to surrender, as well as the information needed to contextualize the first three steps in the 12-step program. This current section is dedicated to providing a continual context for "ah-ha" moments to arise naturally within you, based solely on the truths you're being exposed to in real-time.

Once we understand the need for surrender and the way it works in our life, and once we take the first three steps in earnest, we will have built a foundation of knowingness about surrender that will fuel the rest of the work to be done here, as well as the rest of the work to be done when one chooses to live a spiritual life. The last two sections of this book with regards to the 12-steps are rooted in forgiveness and gratitude.

Surrender, forgiveness, and lastly gratitude, are the three mechanisms we have as localities of consciousness to transcend this world and find God always present. We'll get more into this as we move along, but for now I have to tell you the way to God is straight and narrow, always upwards, and paved with surrender, forgiveness and gratitude.

Now, let's get back to fear and desire and the direct topic at hand, which is understanding these forces, so it becomes easier to let go of our attachment to the beliefs we have they represent reality and not illusion.

Fear and desire are maybe the most common representations of forces in our life that most people on the planet have regular run-ins with. These two forces are also possible motivators for those who find themselves in consciousness levels below these, as the fear of death might spurn someone forward and out of agony. With desire as well as fear we come across the first negative levels of consciousness which can motivate someone to move. Even if the movement is flawed and based on a lie, it still can create movement.

Many people believe both fear and desire to be quality aspects of life, worthwhile emotional states to move from, and overall, two levels of consciousness which feel as if they are 100% part of what it means to be a human. However, those who would believe this are not currently living in these attracter fields as their total reality, and many only have these forces arise within their life from time to time to serve as reminders that they feel cut off from who they want to be most, or what it is they think will create the most happiness in their life.

Fear and desire are no-joke scenarios to find oneself inhabiting as reality. These are also two aspects of consciousness that bring about incredible destruction for the person who resonates here currently, and not just for themselves or even for the whole world around them, but certainly for their inner circle of friends and their chosen work atmospheres.

With fear as the basis for the ego's outward expression, the world looks to be a place worth being scared of, and a place that is best left to be fixed. When someone comes from a place of fear, they have little ability to empathize with another or trust someone else's intentions. This is the case because they have little ability to trust themselves, so how can they trust another? If I am all fear, it is also a likelihood and probability that I lie, cheat and steal in my regular daily activities. It doesn't mean that I tell huge lies, steal large quantities of goods, or cheat on the person whom I'm romantically involved with, but I do lie about my intentions, steal the trust of others, and cheat on myself by allowing other negative forces to become chosen within my regular day-to-day activities.

Desire is a funny little beast of a reality as one's consciousness, because it creates an immense amount of juice for the personal ego, and because of the amount of juice and the self-fulfilling way the ego has the ability to prove itself correct time and time again, desire may be a place better than apathy, but it's a place far from joy.

Desire can lift someone out of grief and shame by refocusing the aim on getting something out in the world to replace how one feels inside. Desire can be a catalyst for seeing the ego more clearly as well, for with desire, one always wants more and continually finds anger close by as the fuel needed for continually not getting what they want.

There have been seasons in my life where I was riddled with fear and constantly overcome with desire. As I look back on my drinking career, there were weeks, if not months, where I regularly stayed stuck in these lesser ways to live. I would fear that the way I was feeling and acting would always be the case, and I would vacillate between being angry with God because of it and desiring something and anything to make it better. As I reflect back on times of fear and desire as being present realities, these two forces are also major players in taking someone from drinking because they enjoy it, to drinking more when they don't.

As someone falls deeper and deeper into being a slave to their ego and the world, they look for anything within the world to make them feel better. As anyone who is/was an alcoholic will tell you, a day lived without a buzz was a day where hell seemed present around every corner. Meaning, if I wasn't drinking, I wasn't escaping my current predicament of misery based in fear and desire. Drinking for many is a pastime which creates an alternate way of experiencing life and the world around them. But for the alcoholic, drinking becomes the only way to experience life because without it they have to come face to face with exactly what it is they're drinking to escape from.

Fear and desire break up relationships, companies, partnerships, bonds, families, and eventually the singular person's entire way of life out in the world who embodies such forces as current levels of consciousness. Out of fear and desire come poor decision making and the propensity to cheat on a partner or lie about their addictions to themselves and the world around them. In these two lower states it's easy to take something or to lie about something if either serves yourself to feel more superior or better than another in the moment. Fear and desire create realities where the person who is either, or who has bouts with either, believes the world is out to get them because how they approach the world is from a desperate place of wantingness as opposed to a place of acceptance.

If someone is truly embodying fear or allowing it to stay around for the foreseeable future, their view of God is as punitive in nature and as if God takes delight in punishing God's creation. Likewise, the way they approach life is as though frightened of it and without love present within their day-to-day experience. The emotional state most common when engulphed with fear is anxiety for the future and decisions to withdrawal from the world in the present. Fear, as a level of consciousness, is the beginning of one fully working all the angles to be alone with misery, whereas desire is mostly being alone but wanting others to make you feel better at the same time. Desire and fear are both places where hell is experienced as a reality. If either of these consciousness levels are where you find yourself currently, or remember resonating with such attracter patterns, you know I'm speaking from firsthand experience.

If someone finds that desire is where they currently reside, they most likely choose to deny the existence of a creator and would consider themselves an atheist without the title needed, and when they look around at their life it feels as though disappointment is all it's worth and they have amounted to nothing, even though they might be quite financially sound or successful as the world would see it. Desire is characterized through an emotional state as craving, and through cravingness the appetite for satisfaction can never be satiated. Desire is lived out through total enslavement to the ego and all of its lower perversions. Desire is also a place that creates only more wanting – with more wanting comes only more wanting. The very act of desiring or wanting is the reward for wanting and desiring more. Desiring something or wanting something doesn't cause that thing to become present, and if you acquire something in this state which you thought would make you happy, once acquiring it you realize you're still not happy and you begin your search for something else to get and have. No amount of money, or homes, or romantic partners, or nights out, or good times had will fill the God-sized hole you have in your heart when calibrating at either fear or desire, or anywhere around or within these levels as well.

New age styled, pseudo gurus, love to mentate about

how desire and fear are quality emotional sets worth employing for getting what it is you want. And in the same breath, they'll say the way they got something was by wanting it or desiring it as well, or by using fear to propel them into a reality where something was manifested for them because of it. This is all nonsense. If you have a current spiritual teacher who uses fear or desire as a means to acquire happiness or places you in situations where fear and desire are the underlying mechanisms for spiritual advancement, look closely at how they're benefiting from this false teaching and you'll see the crux is not based on truth but based on manipulation. It is true, what we hold in mind tends to manifest, but just because we hold something in mind does not mean it materializes for us and comes in a way that brings happiness along with it, and it surely doesn't materialize because we want or desire it.

As was stated previously, both fear and desire seem commonplace for most people alive today, as well as those in the past, but speaking from firsthand experience with these two states of actual levels of prolonged consciousness, these two levels are actually middle levels of hell. At my lowest point of despair, I calibrated between both levels of fear and desire, and it was from this point that my bottom was propelled forth into heaven, as it was at this point that God delivered me from these two body-snatchers of humanity and recused me into to a place that I only look back on now. These two levels of consciousness, while being in them subjectively, were my first glimpses into actual hell as something that felt like eternity. When you reach these levels or have them periodically present themselves into awareness when not calibrating as such totally, it feels as if love is nowhere in sight, and because of love being nowhere around you in a way you can see or feel, this is where one can catch a glimpse of what eternity is. The same is true for states of great love, for in both the up and the down, eternity is found in an instant of either. Fear and desire are only useful for the person who needs to move from further down the scale towards further up the scale. No one has to go through all the levels of consciousness in a linear succession, and there is no benefit to doing that in this lifetime. So, if you find yourself in misery from feeling no sunlight on your face during these times, just know, in an instant of deep surrender, God will rescue you from yourself if you truthfully ask for help. God is never not God.

I do not recommend anyone choosing to visit these realms or spend much time in their presence, but if you do find yourself there and surrounded by what feels like an eternity without sunlight on the soul, do as I did and scream out for help. Don't stay another minute a slave to these forces of the lower mind, and take faith in knowing that I, too, was once there but delivered from such a low point, not by my actions but by the choice to surrender over my lack of power for transcending such conditions.

TRUTHS:

(The Katha Upanishad) *God allowed man to look outward, but in seeing the outer, the inner is ignored. Those who see the eternal, turn their gaze within.*

(The Tao Te Ching) *When the wise man hears of the Way, he tries hard to follow it. When the average person hears of the Way, he tries to keep it, but eventually loses it. When those who are ignorant hear of the Way, they just laugh. If people didn't laugh at it, it wouldn't be the Way.*

(The Gospel of Thomas) *If you think the Kingdom of God is above you, then the birds will find it first. If you think it is in the ocean, then fish will discover it before you do. Look… the Kingdom of God is within you and all around you.*

(The Buddha) *The Way is not in the sky; the Way is in the heart.*

CONTEMPLATING ON TRUTH:

To this day, if someone asks me to do homework or to study for any type of quiz or exam, unless there was previously a lecture about it or I read it somewhere and it relates, or I listen to a podcast regarding the subject, I won't perform well come test day, because studying was never a natural endeavor for me, nor was it something I could force myself to do. My mode of learning throughout formal education, from elementary school through college, was achieved mainly by listening to the teacher or lecturer, thinking in the moment about what was being said and how it relates to my life, then internalizing whatever knowledge I could walk away with, while simultaneously leaving the rest behind me as I moved onto the next part of my day. Looking back, I'm one of the lucky ones, for without knowing it consciously, I'm inclined since birth to look within for my own answers when the time is right, based upon what the world says, but not adopted because the world says it. Every time someone speaks or I sit alone and read, I have a direct and internal knowingness and truth barometer regarding the words in question, and that concoction always points inward towards the source of all information known and unknown. Inward is where I find meaning for the world outside of myself, and inward, deep down under the noise and confusion of past programming, is where I found God resides - - perfectly still and peaceful, always present and never demanding.

Unknown to me since I was a child, I was being prepared for this life in my own unique way, in order to have my own experience of the world around me, just like everyone else on this earth, but only in a unique manner fitting my purpose for inhabiting this particular body in this particular lifetime. Until adulthood, I thought this way of preparation, a non-studying style of learning was laziness on my part, but today I see it as quite the opposite, and as a gift. My perception of reality is formed through internalizing stimuli and equating what is heard and seen into discernment about the incoming data, and then going deep into those inclinations to investigate what's true or false about them. A worthwhile truth found from this exercise came when I realized I'm not just in this world, but this world is in me and it's defined from the inside out. One does not find answers from without that trump what's only answered from within, for out there is but a mirror projecting what's currently found within.

Today, as opposed to times past, I understand the power of choice, and while yesterday I was ignorant to it, today I'm grateful for it. For the most part, we all fluctuate from one polar extreme to the other, from ignorance to wisdom, from sorrow to joy, or from hell to heaven, while experiencing every intermediate aspect of life between and throughout the transition times. Laughing at another out of comparison's sake is an indicator that one is living in a state of ignorance, with ignorance being the first step towards growth. Yesterday, I laughed at others' expense, but today I laugh at myself more than ever, and today I find myself giggling on a regular basis at how beautiful and perfect the Way truly is. Being able to laugh at yourself for comparison's sake is not only an indicator that one is moving towards the Way, but it's part of the intermediate steps taken towards experiencing a new and better subjective reality in your day-to-day life and moment-to-moment existence. Today, I choose to laugh at the Way, and not because it seems foolish as a pursuit, but because of how ignorant I was to see It as anything other than the Ultimate Pursuit.

Throughout my life, I have been a participant in every aspect of life, from ignorance to wisdom, and from wisdom to the absolute average. In fact, we all have. But, in order to follow the Way, you have to be able to laugh at yesterday vs. today for comparison's sake, for today versus yesterday is in fact the demarcation line between the wise and the ignorant. Today, is not a day that needs to be lost to the pursuits of the flesh, instead, today can be filled with wise decisions regarding surrendering over the flesh for the fresh perspective the Way presents. Today, as opposed to yesterday, is what we now have at our fingertips, for yesterday is gone, tomorrow is uncertain, but within the moment of now lies the present, waiting to be unwrapped. Happiness isn't found in ignorance, only momentary glimpses of contentment through false feelings of superiority. If you truly desire happiness, if love is a word you're not sure exists in your everyday life, then it's time to lay aside the childish attempts at remaining saddled with your past. It's now time to let go of past foolishness with regards to hiding from God, and today, the present gift from the creator, you have the opportunity to start laughing at yourself instead of at the world around you.

For most of this lifetime, I imagined I was outside of

the Kingdom of God, while constantly looking for the secret back door that would allow me to slip in unnoticed by its true and worthy inhabitants. And thus, the kingdom of God remained a mystery to me for many years. At times, the Kingdom has been a worthwhile pursuit I looked for out in the world, and at other times it felt as far from my grasp as breathing under water without an oxygen tank. And by thinking that I am somehow separated from the Kingdom of Heaven, I created the boundary that kept me locked outside its gates. However, today I know that the Kingdom of God, the Way, the Path, the Eternal, and any other term one chooses to use for descriptive purposes, is not found above me or below me, it's found within me, hiding in plain sight, but never forcing me to take notice.

By knowing God is found by first looking within, I now know that separation from my Creator is not possible, not even on my worst days, because despite my actions or assumptions, God remains steadfast in position and context. If heaven is found by looking within, it stands to reason that every time we choose to look somewhere else for our connection to God, or to someone else for our definition of God, we're relying on something other than our own inner power to change the world around us. And for me, relying on others to "change my mind," "cure my addictions," or "break my negative habits," is as futile as trying to breathe under water without an oxygen tank. The gift of surrender is the ultimate tool in realizing the possibility of bringing heaven into your life and into your everyday experience of life, and surrender is not found outside of one's self. One does not surrender over life to God so that life will get easier. One surrenders life to God so that the Kingdom of God is able to be entered while moving through the experience of physicality and being a human. Just because we take this human form does not mean we're separated from that which created us, because in fact, what we arise out of we are. There is no separation from what you are, but what you are, maybe you can't see yet, so take the word of someone who's been where you are and spent time in where you want to be, nothing outside yourself will be where you find the Kingdom of God.

The Way is peaceful once you realize it.

The Way is inspirational once you realize it.

The Way is motivating once you realize it.

The Way is beautiful once you realize it.

The Way is perfect once you realize it.

The Way is all-loving once you realize it.

The Way is mighty once you realize it.

The Way is powerful once you realize it.

The Way is everything once you realize it.

The Way is whatever you need it to be once you realize it.

Once I realized the Way was in my heart and not found anywhere else, I finally realized I was beautiful, perfect in reflection, all-loving, motivating, mighty, powerful, peaceful, everything, inspirational, and whatever I need to be in any perfect moment of now, even if I'm not aware of it currently. You see, it's the potential to be all of these things that actualizes once one chooses to move towards the Way. The Way is not a magic pill one takes or a magical elixir for sale out in one of the world's many apothecaries. No, the Way is found within for anyone searching for God, and neither your beliefs nor your actions will have an impact on whether the Way exists or not, as the Way is the context out of which the content of life arises, as well as the content arising.

The Way, the Truth, the Life. These are not about finding yourself as a separate part of the journey, they're about following someone who's been there before telling you that by following their example of looking within for truth, you now know the key ingredient for coming face-to-face with God along the Way.

The Way is narrow indeed but paved with gold once one realizes it. One can be lost at times on their way to Truth, but the Way is always available for any traveler looking for a home with a sturdy foundation. The Way is not found in the sky as the Buddha enlightened us about, it is in fact found by the traveler who chooses introspection and surrender over sailing through the atmosphere aimlessly and without clearance for landing. The Way is a choice. It is a subjective reality. It is truth and also a personal journey and shared experience. Choose to pursue the Way and you'll soon find yourself carried away by the love it provides, and then you'll know it is about finding yourself as part of the Way, as well as being the Way yourself for others to follow.

INSTRUCTIONS FOR STEP THREE:

Find a quiet space away from the noise of other people and from the busyness of the world. If you find yourself making it to this step and you cannot escape what's around you and you're ready to take this step, don't worry about where you are, just close your eyes for a moment or two and take a few deep breaths to begin. This step can be taken by speaking the words below internally or externally, but I would recommend doing both in succession and then writing them down after you're finished reciting them.

What this step means, is that you are making a decision

to surrender your life over to a power greater than yourself, for the purpose of having a life you're not sure exists. This step is the definition of faith, and by taking this step you are making an act of faith to divinity and the world around you. This is an action step of surrender, and it is also the very step that if taken in earnest, will change your life for years to come in ways you cannot even fathom yet. Do not take this step without much self-reflection and without knowing that your life will change from the moment you take this step. The true spiritual life of surrender starts once this step is taken, because once your life is surrendered over to God, it might change drastically and be rearranged to fit a higher will for you as opposed to your will for you.

This step is the last of three in the surrender section of this book, with the previous two steps setting the context for this one here about to be taken. Many people are not aware that a spiritual life can be what the world calls a messy life, and that a truly spiritual life is not all rainbows and sunshine, because to be aware of a rainbow one first has to weather the storm. This step invites God into your life in a way that will recontextualize your very existence. This step is not to be taken lightly, for if you take it, your life will most assuredly look different moving forward, and at times feel totally out of control, but without giving up your will in exchange for a higher will for you, transcending fear and the personal ego will not be possible.

The life of Truth is straight and narrow, and few choose to traverse it to the end because it's not an easy one by the world's measure. However, a life fueled by pursuing Truth is the only adventure worth taking, for how will you know who God is and what you are while still remaining attached to the beliefs that come from something smaller than that which created it?

The answer to that question is found within this step and what comes next after taking it.

Best of luck to all who have read these words and endeavor to persevere into the truth that Love has in store for you. Many blessings on a life worth living and journey worth sharing that is about to become evident to those who move past this step and into step four with an honest and open heart for truth.

STEP THREE

-

I make the decision here and now, to turn my will and life over to Thee oh Lord. I choose love in the face of fear, your power instead of the forces of the ego, and I accept grace as a gift I don't fully understand.

STEP THREE PRAYER

-

I surrender over this life, my control over it, my desire to control it, the belief I'm in control of it, and my wantingness for life to go the way I want it to go and still reach truth in the end. Truth is surrendered over as I see it in exchange for Truth that can only be experienced, witnessed and observed from your lens.

SECTION TWO

-

Chapters 4 - 9

-

Forgiveness

Chapter 4

TRANSCENDING THE FORCES
OF ANGER & PRIDE
The gift of an examined life...

The three-step process to finding one's way to God is simple, and so simple that most in history have missed it: surrender, forgiveness, gratitude. These three action steps are also what comprises the 12-step program found here in this book. As I was going through the 12-steps myself for overcoming an addiction to alcohol, I wasn't aware at the time that these were the synthesis of the steps in succession, but as I made my way towards completion of the steps and looked back on them with an open heart and a clearer mind, I saw that all of the 12 steps fell within these categories.

Over the years and since finishing the steps for myself, through regular prayer, periodic meditation and continued contemplation, what arose as truth is that by following a pathway where surrender, forgiveness and gratitude are at the center of it, one comes face to face with truth in uncompromising ways. If you earnestly surrender over the lesser for the greater, forgive yourself, God, others, and the world for how you feel wronged or how you feel you wronged another, and then actively embrace gratitude for a life free of thinking you're the worst aspects of your mind, you'll find God in abundance waiting there. And you too will have the realization that it wasn't that Love just showed up, it's that you finally woke up to the fact that God was and is always there with an abundance of love present.

Anger and pride are two stumbling blocks that everyone on earth is familiar with, as well as accustomed to the after-effects of both characteristics of the ego. There is not a person alive who has not felt both of these aspects of humanity arise within them at least once in their life, and more accurately though, arise many, many times in their life, perhaps even once a day. Speaking from an American standpoint, based in the basic psychology and parameters of success that is indoctrinated when growing up a U.S. citizen, both anger and pride are seen as quality aspects worth embracing and not surrendering.

Anger and pride as aspects of being a human are experienced all the time by many, but actually having a consciousness level of either anger or pride, or falling somewhere in-between, are altogether different scenarios entirely.

As Dr. Hawkins states in his map of consciousness, if one finds themselves in a lower level of consciousness than anger and pride, these two aspects of the lower mind can be motivators for success and for upward mobility. However, they always end in damaging ways for the person who uses both energies as a means to an end. When someone finds themselves at the levels of anger or pride as inhabitable levels of consciousness, they vacillate between seeing God as vengeful to indifferent. Meaning, if I am angry with the world and I regularly don't get what I want, my way of seeing the creator is also how I see myself, which is out to get at all costs. When one reaches a level of pride as their resting point, they are so consumed with their worth versus the worth of another, that they don't have time for God and in turn see the creator through the lens of "who really cares?"

Within these levels of consciousness, the practitioner of both has a life-view of either antagonistic towards the world or too demanding for getting what they want, or a mixture of both repeatedly as they survey the world and how it operates against them. At the level of anger, it's easy to hate another person, whereas at the level of pride that hate moves more into judgment and scorn. Anger also gives way to aggression, whereas pride gives rise to the embodiment of an inflated sense of self. Both experiences of anger and pride are also the byproducts of drunkenness many times, as well as where someone might find their state of awareness after being consumed with lust for another or the wanting of something without getting it.

Neither anger nor pride are fun levels to find oneself currently residing in, and if you do find that the characteristics of both are declarative of where you are and how you see things currently, just know that you're headed towards a mighty fall if you don't surrender these over to God immediately. Again, having anger and pride arise as temporary experiences is normal. This doesn't mean you're backsliding towards a life of despair. It just means the ego is presenting itself in a way that is beneficial for you knowing what needs to be surrendered over in the moment to move past whatever issues seem to be present at the time. If you find yourself as anger or pride continually, take faith in the knowingness that I, too, was once these levels of consciousness, but through surrendering them over to a power greater than myself, these levels subsided and gave way to genuine happiness and gratitude for existence.

This chapter is all about the 4th step in the program, and I would be remiss if I did not break it down for you now, as well as share the pitfalls that will present themselves in relation to reaching this step and seeing it through until its conclusion. Transcending past anger and moments of pride is what this step is all about, as well as transcending all other aspects of the ego in your quest for finding your own experience with truth.

If anyone is going to quit working the program, it probably will be at this step. If not here, then step 9. Step 4 is also the step that has the potential to bring about the most relief from the ego once completed. It is no coincidence that when one chooses to put their life down on a piece of paper, as is being asked in this step, looking for the ways that being wronged had more to do with the part they played than what the world around them did, the ego feels the most threatened. When the ego feels threatened it tends to lash out through turning up the dials of wants, desires, cravings, procrastination, and any other manner of inner turmoil at its disposal. This is normal and natural, and as we talked about in earlier parts of this book, from a mile-high view the ego does not do this as a means to hurt you, even though it may seem that way when you're going through it. No, it acts in this manner to deliver you along the pathway of knowing what needs to be surrendered and forgiven so that gratitude is a natural state and not something you pretend to have.

In my own experience of the 4th step, I found relief immediately in applying the rules of the step to only a single person, my mother. Because of the relief I felt from the truth of seeing through my clouded past view of our relationship and her role in my life, I felt lighter and more capable of seeing the truth in other aspects of life. I let a little truth with regards to my mom stop me from completing the rest of this step for over a month. This is normal for anyone working through this step, and either you find immediate relief, or you find fears screaming loud enough that it stops the spiritual aspirant from moving through this step as fast as they can or are capable of.

As an aside, many believe the spiritual life and the path to truth to be one always paved in gold and easily traversed every moment of the journey, complete with robes worn and people bowing at your feet for wisdom. However, those are false assumptions. The reason most people never reach a level of consciousness characterized as enlightenment, is not because it is impossible to do in a single lifetime, but because finding God as the reality of Self does not happen through half measures and little effort put forth, nor your clothes worn or fancy breathing techniques. Paraphrasing Jesus, the path is straight and narrow, and it is harder for a rich man to enter the kingdom of heaven than a camel to pass through the eye of a needle. From past experience, this is true. This is not the case because a rich man has done something wrong to become rich, but because serving two masters leads not to enlightenment but to the partial service of both heaven and earth. The road is straight and narrow because in order to find truth and arrive in heaven subjectively while in the physical form, one has to be willing to surrender over their attachment to everything they believe is real, and in turn have faith that the juice which comes from letting go of the world is worth the squeeze of the effort, all while letting go of even the desire to reach enlightenment in the process.

No one can do the work for you to reach higher levels of realized truth, and likewise, no person can give you enlightenment as well – not a guru, teacher, pastor or new age spiritual healer. If someone claims to possess the ability to give you enlightenment, they themselves are far from someone worth investing time into. Enlightenment is a chosen path and one that doesn't always end in finding God as the Self in the lifetime you choose to pursue it. By honestly doing the steps in this book you have the opportunity to undue past karma, to transcend your attachment to the mind, and to see all fears for what they are: illusions. But the work in this book can only take you to the doorway of transcendence. It will be up to you and your karmic propensity for being here as to whether or not you have the last bit of strength needed to rely on God with total surrender and lay down even your life before the Creator. This program will deliver the lost into levels of consciousness where more and more love is present, and if you follow the steps of surrender, forgiveness and gratitude, they can lead you to a level of love or unconditional love as byproducts. Enlightenment is between you and God. Being love is between you and the world.

The aim of this book and the author who pens this work is to point you in the direction of Truth while giving you the tools necessary to choose Love for yourself. As we dive deeper into the rest of the book past this chapter, we'll see together how gratitude is also an action as well as a reality. For now, if you desire and choose to continue chasing after God and moving towards experiencing a life you never thought possible but always hoped could be present, finish this chapter and don't do as I did by putting off finishing the step. But instead, finish the 4th step as quickly as possible without hurrying or missing anything. Be quick, but don't hurry. And don't let the fear of not being perfect stop you from finishing the step.

This step is about being thorough, about being absolutely honest with yourself, and it's not about leaving anything out of the equation. What one leaves out of the equation for dissection is the very same thing the foundation of the ego will find solace in and continue to torment you over. This step brings about fear for many people because they hold onto the mind's belief that looking back at your life in earnest will lead to too much pain and suffering as the result. This assumption couldn't be further from the truth. Why the ego puts up such a fight while approaching this step is because when a person puts pen to paper and breaks down their life as if a movie script, the person starts to truly see the ego as something other than what they are, because they see that what they think and how they think about something is often times far from the truth. This step is not to be done in the mind alone by simply answering some questions internally, for that which you keep in the mind stays fed by the mind, with the mind being the very same thing that writing something down proves to help transcend. We want to get out of the mind in order to better see the mind. There is pure magic in writing things down for this step, and you will not find maximum relief and transcendence if you choose to think you'll be fine by doing this step without a pen and paper. For those of you who choose to not use pen and paper for this step, please put this book on a shelf right now and come back to it when you are ready.

The truth that you'll see in this step is that forgiveness for yourself and the world around you is the byproduct of honestly finishing this step. You'll see that ignorance is the only sin available to mankind, and that if you could have done better you would have done better. You'll also see that it's foolish to hold onto the definitions you gave to past moments in your life once you see them more clearly with the gift of honest and thorough hindsight.

You cannot move on in the steps until this particular step is complete. I'm going to say that one more time: you cannot move on in the steps until this step is complete. If you are unwilling to complete this step before moving on, please put this book on a shelf right now and come back to it when you are ready.

Because of this fact, and because of the way the ego will interact with your awareness while approaching and working on the 4th step, this may be the first time in your life where you'll actually have to choose and practice faith. That's right, faith. Faith is part of the straight and narrow pathway to Truth, but many of you have probably never come across a good description of faith, so let's end this part of the dialogue before we get into further truths in the next section. Talking about faith in a way that might finally feel worthy of understanding and applying.

On July 4th, 2017, I had to choose faith in response to God's offer of help. I had to choose to believe there is a better way of life other than what I currently knew as reality, even though my reality was all that felt real or possible. The way I approached it was through reason at first, meaning: if all of life appears to have an up as well as a down, a left as well as a right, a here as well as a there, wouldn't it stand to reason that if life sucks so bad now, can't it also be wonderful later? That was my bridge to faith before actually choosing faith. Sanity was found in that reasoning for me, and it was through a bit of sanity that I was able to choose faith in the proposition from God about choosing another way to live. From the logic of "just because I feel this way right now and don't truly know that life could be better, doesn't mean that there is not a world where life is better, because for every down there's an up, right?" was the link between choice and faith I needed. Faith, for me, at first, was choosing to trust that there was an up without any evidence of it currently being present.

Faith for you in the face of the 4th step might be something similar: "I have a program and a person who speaks from firsthand experience of the benefits of completing the fourth step and the program as a whole, so am I going to believe my ego which says I don't need to complete it, or am I going to have faith that once it's thoroughly completed and the steps are finished, I will have the hindsight and relief needed to know that faith is actually part of the pathway to transcending the very same thing that tried to convince me otherwise?"

Faith at first is a choice, but the wonderful thing about faith is that it breeds more faith, and with more and more faith one has the opportunity to have faith as a habitual response to life. Once faith becomes part of what you are, God is not out of reach for long. Faith in action is the quickest way to transcend the mind and see truth more clearly. Most people choose what they presently understand and are comfortable with as opposed to the choice of having faith that there has to be something better than what they're currently experiencing, especially if what one is currently experiencing has caused them to even question if there's a way to actually be happy. Do you see how faith is a choice to start with logic and reason and end with taking a calculated leap? If you know you're not happy, why would you choose to double down on where you are and what you know (even though it's creating no growth) as opposed to having faith that there's something else out there ready to be experienced?

If you find yourself stuck in completing the 4th step, take stock in what I am about to say: all fear is an illusion, and it is perfectly safe to walk straight through it. Faith without action is worthless in this case, for it takes faith to have the action necessary to see that faith was part of what set you free. Once you have your own experience of faith, you'll be able to provide another with hope when they need it, and just like truth, faith is a gift that one can't talk about from firsthand experience without having firsthand experience with it. Having faith in the fact that you are not greater than that which created you also leads to the humility needed to honestly give an appraisal of your life in this step which is the whole reason we're doing this step. Faith in something greater than you is not foxhole fear or weakness. In all actuality it's strength. The ability to admit one's limitations and then ask for help with them is anything but weakness.

TRUTHS:
(The Tao Te Ching) *Achieve the state of a new-born child. Clear and purify inner vision.*

(The Gospel of John) *Unless one is born anew, he cannot see the Kingdom of God.*

(The Dhammapada) *With earnest meditation, purity of mind, and compassionate acts of kindness, you will become an island of serenity which even the greatest floods cannot sweep away.*

(The Bhagavad Gita) *See Me in all things. Dwell in Me as I dwell in you.*

CONTEMPLATING ON TRUTH:
Whether you grew up in a faith-based household or grew up without the thought of religion entering your psyche, one can agree that the eyes of a child are filled with wonder, excitement, enthusiasm, and unfiltered love for those who show love first, not based upon a religion, but intrinsic to their molecular make-up.

Children are magical beings, filled with no animosity towards another race, ethnicity, gender or species apart from themselves. But at a certain point they begin to be programmed by their surroundings and by those who raise them to think otherwise, and often remain tightly connected to the people and the world views around them. Children are inherently innocent from birth, only knowing that which they are taught, besides the sensations of hunger, warmth, the need to use the bathroom, and love from their caregivers. When we transition into adulthood, we have become mannequins clothed by others' ideas of the world, and the garments we wear are direct reflections of how we were told to see the world around us. The key to letting go of both the programs of anger and pride is as simple as surrendering over our past programming, one layer at a time, to a power greater than ourselves, until we reach a place of purified inner vision towards the world around us. That does not mean we become naive to the ways of the world, but we instead become open to a different reality not yet held by our ego-driven conceptions of what we have come to believe reality is.

In some degree of truth, from one angle, reality is subjectively what we say it is, and only our perception of it gives rise to any particular definition. So, the same amount of energy it takes to be angry with a stimulus is the same amount of energy it takes to love a stimulus. What was educated into us can be unlearned, reprogrammed, and reconstructed from the ground up if need be; all depending on the world we choose to live in once we separate from the throws of childhood programming. The world is inherently nothing more than the world, and it is neither bad nor good, it just is. What we see in the world is dependent on our level of consciousness, and our level of consciousness is dependent on our willingness to surrender the lesser definition for the greater awareness. Anger and pride are both aspects of the ego personified. And when one remains in lockstep with the personal ego, one remains a slave to both anger and pride. Life is better when one surrenders the ego for the state of a new-born child, complete with clear and purified inner vision.

Being born anew is not a religious term but more of a daily spiritual way of experiencing the world. Depending on your religious background, the term "born again," or "born anew," may carry significant weight or turmoil for the person looking the shed anger and pride from their life. However, both terms simply give the spiritual seeker a starting point for their new journey of self-discovery, regardless of their predisposition within the confines of a current mode of thinking or religious dogma. One cannot move from where they are to where they have the potential to be without first knowing from where it is they are starting. One cannot build a mighty structure atop a wobbly foundation, and then think the building will stand for years to come. If the foundation is unknown and untested, the building atop it won't last for long. One cannot experience the joy and freedom that comes from transcending anger and pride until they first choose to start again by being born anew and start again from a place of purified emptiness as well as renewed emphasis on keeping a fixed gaze on the Kingdom of God.

In order to see the glory of the Kingdom of God, which is in and around you, one must choose first to acknowledge that their outer life is but a mirror of an inner level of consciousness. And if so chosen, can be cleansed for a fresh start by letting go of perpetual negative programming through the process of surrender. Being born anew simply means, to wake up in the moment of now and realize that in this very moment there is the chance, as well as the opportunity, to start fresh with a completely different perspective, renewed hope, and a refreshed emphasis on living consciously. In essence, being born anew means that from the rebirth forward, a new direction is continually chosen by the chooser and not burdened by past habits. Every moment we are born anew, but very few choose to see the opportunities that this revelation produces in the precise moment of choosing in the here and now.

When one chooses to look outside of themselves for happiness instead of within for the Kingdom of God, they're choosing to ignore the opportunity to be born anew. Whenever someone chooses to pursue validation through the eyes of another instead of through internally seeking the Kingdom of God, they're choosing to ignore the opportunity to be born anew. With every choice comes the opportunity to be born again.

Anger and pride scoff at earnest meditation, and then retort with 'why should I meditate, I am fine the way I am?'

Anger and pride scoff at purity of mind, and then retort with "why do I need to purify my mind, it is fine the way it is?"

Anger and pride scoff at compassionate acts of kindness, and then retort with "why should I help that person, no one helped me?"

Anger and pride like to scoff at all things seemingly opposite of their attracter energies because the last thing anger and pride desire to do is vanish from your life. In fact, anger and pride carry along with them more anger and further moments of conceited behavior which beckon opportunities to show the world what they're made of.

Anger and pride, as they arise, act as if they are your dearest friends of old, but unlike a true friend who is in your life to be a benefit and a blessing, anger and pride have no other motivation than that of destruction and separation. As a man who once lived his life dominated by lesser attracter fields, consumed by both pride and anger, and now as the same physical entity, yet transformed by surrendering both over to God, I can bear witness to the fact that happiness immediately followed the latter rendition of the man who now writes to you today.

Holding onto anger and pride does nothing but cast away the sunshine from your face, acting as a distraction of needless clouds carrying with them distant hopes of better days to come.

Anger and pride cannot test the strength of an island built with a foundation of Love, but they will do their best to hide the promise of its beaches from any would-be island hopper. When one allows anger or pride to play a dominant role in their day-to-day life, what they're essentially doing is allowing their life to be less impactful than it could be, less meaningful than it could be, and less important than it is. The importance of a man is not measured by how many enemies he makes, or even defeats, but by how many people he helps.

Anger and pride will not allow you to help another person as easily as a life where anger and pride are surrendered over for the gifts of love and acceptance. Anger and pride are two parts of the ego manifested, embraced, and chosen if allowed to remain dominant points of perspective. One misses the gifts that freedom carries with it when they remain a slave to the cravings of resentment and adulation which are by-products of anger and pride.

When we choose to take on a different viewpoint of life, and when we choose to be born anew in the Love and

Power of the Way, we not only understand that the Kingdom of God resides within our very beingness, but we also see that anger and pride are nothing more than two levels of consciousness designed to help the spiritual seeker choose the greater of two paths possibly traveled. When I found myself dominated by anger and pride, I felt as if there was no way out, no way to have a better life where happiness was part of the equation. The willpower that was mine at the time had failed to produce a life that was worth living. Until I let go of both anger and pride and surrendered over my attachments to both, life appeared as nothing more than existing day-to-day. Suddenly, upon the final surrendering of both anger and pride, the clouds parted above my head and I not only knew I could find a new life dwelling in the Lord, but that the Lord had been dwelling within me the entire time. God is in all things, what language calls the good and the bad, but it took seeing anger and pride as nothing more than opportunities to learn this lesson, until I understood what lesson I was to learn in the first place. You see, anger and pride are levels along an evolutionary scale of consciousness. It just so happens to be one's level of consciousness that dictates how one views the world around them, how one loves themselves, and how one views God and the world at large.

If you stay stuck in the juice of anger and pride, you miss out on the pleasures of love and acceptance that lay hidden on the other side of letting go of your attachments to both negative energy fields. Anger and pride are particular attracter fields, but both anger and pride carry very little power along with them to create happiness as a lasting reality. When anger and pride are seen as teaching agents and only aspects of the experience of being human, and not what a person is when they both arise, there is hope for transcending these aspects of the personal ego experience, and thusly of moving into a more conscious connection with that which created you. The parts of clouds that hide a person from the sunlight of the spirit are the particulates known as anger and pride. As long as one holds onto their attachment to either, the spiritual traveler stays stuck in the rain and remains a safe distance from regular sunshine.

INSTRUCTIONS FOR STEP FOUR:

We first begin by making a list of all the people, places, things and institutions we currently carry resentments of, fear over, or anger towards. Be exhaustive in this list and vigilant not to leave out anything for the sake of shame. This list is your list, and it's not my list or the world's list. This initial list is what you'll use to complete the worksheet designed to walk you through what to do with the list compiled. For this part of the step, I would take out a piece of paper and a pen and write at the top of the page the title of the list, i.e., people, or places, things or institutions. Once you have a title for the page, write a short prayer underneath saying something to the effect of: Lord, please help me see what needs to be seen so that I can surrender over what needs to be surrendered over.

If you're like I was and feel as if there are no current resentments or active fears coming to mind, feel free to create your list, but start by also placing a number corresponding with an age below the prayer and let God show you at that age what comes up when sitting down to write the list out. I started with 1, and made my way to 32, with not every year yielding information worth writing down. But to my astonishment, many aspects of early life came back into awareness as a result and then I wrote them down as they came up. My list at the end of this looked like 32 years' worth of information regarding people, places, things and institutions. No matter how you get your initial list of people, places, things and institutions written down, the goal is to have a complete list to work with for the rest of the step.

Feel free to use the worksheet as part of the references in this book, or you can find worksheets all over the internet which will be helpful once you have the list created and are ready to apply it. But whatever worksheet you find to help with this step, it needs to comprise at least 4 basic elements:

1. Category one: The person, place, thing, institution
2. Category two: The offense needing investigation
3. Category three: Affects my … self-esteem, personal relationships, material possessions, finances, ambitions, and sex relations
4. Category four: Where was I to blame … selfish, dishonest, self-seeking, frightened, and inconsiderate.
    -   2nd part of category four: The exact nature of my wrong

If you decide to use the worksheet in this book, or once you have found a worksheet online that fits the parameters above, print off a copy of it and be ready to make many more copies for future use.

Once the people, places, things and institutions aspects of your list is complete, there is one last inventory which needs to be addressed: the sexual inventory. In this area of the step, we look back over all past sexual encounters we have taken part in over the course of our lives. This section of the step accounts for acts of sex, partners with sexual encounters, as well as times of lusting we took part in throughout our life. We also look at the use of pornography and any other behaviors we keep locked away out of sight for the world to see. When I comprised my list for this component of the 4th step, I blocked people into categories of relationships, short flings, one-night stands, encounters other than intercourse that were nameless, and attachments to people whom I was having sex with. Remember, this step is yours, not the world's, so whatever you share with yourself is what you share with God, and then inevitably with someone you trust to be confidential in the 5th step.

We will go deeper into the reason for the 5th step in the next chapter, but please don't be less than thorough in your sexual inventory because you fear that someone will find out and be mad at you, or because you think God or someone else will judge you. Everyone on earth who goes through these steps accounts for all manner of quirky sexual encounters, and whatever your proclivity for sexual arousal is, it is not something someone else hasn't gone through or had experience with. You are not unique in your sexual encounters, and your sexual encounters are not worth hiding behind for fear that releasing them isn't a worthwhile endeavor.

This step is designed to allow someone to look back over their life and examine it from a clearer headspace. If you have experienced sexual trauma in your past, abuse in your past, cultish programming in your past, or any other form of abuse which is still fresh to you or has not had the opportunity to be worked through in any other manner by you to date, know that you are not at fault for any circumstances of what has transpired, and also know that by looking back over past traumatic experiences, there is a chance that the wound will feel fresh again. This process is not designed to bring you pain and anguish, so if digging up certain past traumas on your own is not comfortable or safe for you to do, feel free to bring in an experienced counselor or therapist to help you with this step.

You also have the benefit of attending an open AA meeting on the steps which could help you understand more clearly their intent and how to work through them. If you attend a meeting or meetings, which I encourage you to do, do not speak if the opportunity arises for you to do so, simply say "I pass" or "I am here to observe and learn, so I pass." 12-step groups have open and closed meetings, with the open meetings being for anyone who desires to attend, and the closed meetings being for only those who suffer with the disease they are there to learn more about. You can look up meetings in your area online and you will see brief descriptions of them posted there as well. Within the description of the meeting, you will see if it is closed or open. All meetings and the people within them are anonymous, which means what you see and hear in there stays in there. You are never to out another person for being in a meeting, nor do you bring attention to such people when out in public as being part of an anonymous group. It is more than okay to say hello to the people you meet in meetings when out in the world and to build lasting friendships and relationships with them, but anonymity is the basis for these rooms of healing.

In any 12-step program there is the added benefit of having a sponsor who has gone through the steps to show you how to go through them. This book can act as your pseudo sponsor, as well as the online lectures about the steps you'll find littered about on the internet, and the lectures I will have on the internet every week talking about the steps and walking people through them. As more people complete these steps with the aid of a sponsor, more sponsors will become available to help take you through the steps and be ready for you to take the 5th step.

As part of this book's mission, and part of the author's reason for existence, through online platforms, at least one day a week is devoted to the 12-step program for transcending the ego and fear. As our community grows, so too will availability of sponsors. If you cannot find a sponsor through our program, feel free to ask a trusted friend, religious figure in your life, counselor or therapist to stand in for the 5th step and parts of the 4th step. Remember, sponsors are only guides to the program and not your savior or your way to finding salvation. A sponsor is not to be given money or helped out financially for giving you their time. If someone asks you for money to be taken through the steps, politely say no and choose never to think of them again as someone trusted to help you with the 12-steps.

To date, I have been through this program myself, I have witnessed hundreds of others go through the program, and I have taken multiple people through it as well. By the time this book is published there will be more people who have gone through the program, as well as online resources designed to help people with the program. You are not alone in this pursuit and the benefits of such, and you will not be alone in working these steps whenever they find you.

STEP FOUR

-

I choose to make a fearless and searching moral inventory of
my life, leaving out nothing of consequence.

STEP FOUR PRAYER

-

Please help me to see what needs to be seen in order to
surrender over what needs to be surrendered. Thank you for
the gift of truth, and for the gift of faith in a power greater
than myself restoring me to a life transcendent over the ego.

Chapter 5

EXPERIENCING COURAGE

I was ready for a change…

There is a shift of perception and consciousness that happens once someone has the humility to admit to themselves, and to God, that they in fact are in need of help. The personal ego has an innate belief structure within it that it is in fact god, so it is not a natural proclivity for those still a total slave to the ego to admit they are not the center of the universe in the ways they believe to be true.

During my most ardent days of falling well short of having love present with any regularity, I would search for hope in places where the wells were dry and the spigots turned off. I would look for joy in the arms of a new lover, hope in the presence of a new job, love in a fun night out, and overall definitions for life in some self-help book written by yet another person that claims to have the answers. And for a higher price I could actually hear it in person. For an additional charge, even walk away with an autograph. Our physical world and all of its content is nothing more than a grand display of the ego, with our attachments presenting varying degrees of enslavement to it. From the television we watch to the religious services we attend, the people we interact with, the books we read, the conversations we have, and on and on and on it goes. All roads in the world lead to just more roads in the world, all without providing the traveler a trustworthy compass.

All of the searching for God out in the world, and more precisely, all of the hiding I did out in the world hoping God wouldn't notice, amounted to a well of information about where Love is not found in abundance. I'm not saying that God is not out in the world for all to see, or in our church services and self-help teachings, but the world and the content of the world is but a smaller fraction of the aspect of God we call consciousness. And if we settle for the world as opposed to push for our own experience with God, we'll always remain in a constant state of searching without ever finding. In fact, the world is created in some ways to be a place which creates perpetually the ability to constantly search without finding, to seek without discovering, and to think without true thoughts.

Consciousness is the backdrop of life and all experience, and it is the same thing as what the bible and other religious texts refer to as God's greatest characteristics: omniscience, omnipotence, and omnipresence. As was stated earlier in the book, consciousness can be broken down into levels of abstraction and subjective perception which Dr. David R. Hawkins discovered and spent the latter half of his life lecturing about and teaching on. I have found the levels of consciousness to be worth their weight in gold for contextualizing how this world works and how/why everything happens, from seeming randomness to calculating exact reactions of another based on where they calibrate currently. The levels of consciousness are a major indicator of context for the writing of this book, but they are not what this book is about. They are only further moments of deeper understanding as to what happens within the individual as they grow closer to truth or fall further away from it. The levels of consciousness are nothing more than a map of how life works within the confines of spiritually looking at the great expanse of creation through evolution. (Note: creation and evolution are one in the same.)

As I found relief in surrendering over to God powerlessness with an alcohol addiction, I also found an understanding of what was taking place within my being as following the exact levels of consciousness discussed by Dr. Hawkins. At first, once looking at his map, I didn't know how accurate it was or even what it meant, but as I evolved upwards, it not only provided a context for what was happening to me, but I started to pay attention to how accurate it was for contextualizing every aspect of a rapidly changing life. The levels he describes are not a religion or even a belief system. They are a quantifiable way to understand life and how it works regardless of our awareness of it at any point in time. So far in this book, we have spent time working towards transcending lower levels of consciousness through the acts of varying degrees of surrender, and most recently moved into a realm of forgiveness being the meat of discussion for steps four and five. As I found a way to understand what was taking place as a consequence of working the steps through the map of consciousness, this step can be likened to that by seeing the "ah-ha" moments that arose from step four and by coming face to face with the "ah-ha" moments which will be a result of successfully completing step five.

All of this book has made its way to the moment at hand where we move from transcending the lower levels of the ego and start understanding how the ego persists through the integrous realms of existence starting with the level of courage. Once one finds that courage is the underpinning of their experience of life, they have transcended fear in all of its forms. By transcending fear, I do not mean the spiritual aspirant no longer experiences forms of fear or lesser ego states, but one is no longer a slave to the ego and all the forms of fear it has at its disposal. Once someone has surrendered over their life to God and has earnestly taken the first three steps of this book, there is no possible way they have not transcended fear. If you integrously take the first three steps of this book, you are at the very least operating from a level of courage or above. The first three steps require brutal honesty, and it's in the brutal honesty that you first find God. And because of brutal honesty, you now have the opportunity to come from a place of courage rather than from a lower ego state. Why this is important is because if you don't do Step One perfectly, and by perfectly we mean with absolute honesty, Steps Two and Three become just a formality, and you continue to just blow smoke.

Where we find ourselves now in relation to the steps, is at a place where forgiveness begins for the self and the world around us through step four, and then gets to take on new steam and significance through the working of step five where we see naturally that forgiveness for everything is the key to experiencing more and more love. This step is where we get to see courage in action, as well as the gifts of the spirit which come from a lightened load with regards to all the baggage we carried for so long, now being let go of, creating lighter steps forward. Forgiveness is about letting God handle the grudges, the resentments, the angers and pains, and because of this we have a way through these steps as an actionable witness to this happening without having to do any of the heavy lifting.

When one reaches a level of courage, they take on a whole new attitude about God, life, their circumstances, emotional states, and how they interact with the world. Through Dr. Hawkins's map of consciousness, we see that once courage is present as one's level of consciousness, their view of the creator is one of being permitting of change for the better of the individual, almost as if they now feel like God is allowing them to experience grace and blessings. Their life-view has now shifted from demanding more of the world to satiate their appetite, to one where positive change and a better life feels feasible and within their grasp. Words of affirmation become powerful motivators for those calibrating closely to courage, and their entire outlook on life and how they process the world becomes one of empowerment as opposed to inflation of the ego.

The same reflection of change in one's personal outlook on the world through Dr. Hawkins's map of consciousness once reaching courage, is the same thing happening in the 5th step of this program: the practitioner leaves the world of carrying around past baggage and finds that they have reached a destination where it's okay if their bags were lost during the trip. The 5th step is where we unburden ourselves of what we uncovered about our self and the life we lived up until this point, and also where we begin to see that forgiveness is the gift which creates the context for experiencing gratitude as a reality and not as something needing to be faked.

In this step, the person working the steps shares with someone who has completed the steps, all that was found as a byproduct of their searching and fearless moral inventory. The person who has the honor of listening to the finished fourth step is as blessed to be a part of the process as the blessings that will soon flow into the life of the person who performed their fourth step. The relationship between the talker and the listener in this phase of the program is mutually healing and cathartic and is another example of actively choosing faith through surrendering over the enslavement to inner fears brought on by the personal ego.

As was stated earlier, if there is not someone in your life who can be the partner to your fourth step, and listen to you unload all that you have found, look to a priest, pastor, Imam, close friend and confidant, a parent, your therapist or counselor for aid in finishing this step. To complete the fifth step, all you have to do is admit out loud to yourself, to God, and to another human being, the exact nature of your wrongs which you found by working the fourth step – it's that simple. Within the Big Book of Alcoholics Anonymous, and I'm paraphrasing, it is stated that you will be amazed and feel a lightness of being before the steps are finished, and because of the magic of steps 1-4, when you get to step five, if you haven't felt life shift for you or you haven't had your perceptions of life change yet, be ready for a major "ah-ha" moment to arise from finding yourself speaking out loud to another what you found binding about your life to date.

What we hold inside tends to bring about pain because to keep the past hidden and locked away we hold traumas and mistruths as precious to us, or too painful to embrace and let go of. What happened to us in our past happened to us in our past. What happened to us in our past was moments in time we've already survived. What happened to us in our past are examples of the strength and resiliency of being in human form, but just because we have a past doesn't mean it's worth being attached to any longer.

The aspect of this step that holds the potential for such relief and such a lightness of being, is in saying out loud to another as well as to God simultaneously, what we once hid and used to define our view of ourselves as being separate from the world around us, is now worth letting go of for a new vantage point moving forward. When you share with another person your baggage, you get an immediate understanding through the interaction that they too have shared in some of the same baggage, which only serves to bring the fourth-stepper closer to the realization that they are not alone, nor are they someone who should continue believing they are any longer.

Just like writing the fourth step down on paper, we share the fifth step out loud so our mind is not the final destination where truth can be limited or have an opportunity for manipulation. When we open up to another about who we are and what we've done, the direct result is choosing faith over fear, openness over hiding, honesty over deception, and truth over manipulation.

This particular step signifies something massively important and unique for all of those brave enough to get to this point, which is a display to ourselves and to God that in fact we have chosen Truth over falsehood, Power over force, Salvation over skepticism, Joy over pain, and Life over death.

If you take a moment at this point in the program to survey what has transpired since starting this work, what you'll find, at the very least, is someone who prayed to God or maybe asked the universe for help with life, for help with some aspect of life, with that prayer or request being answered in the form of what you're doing now. You have made it this far in the book and are more than halfway done with regards to the effort needed to finish the steps. You have done something in working steps 1-4 that very few people in the halls of time have had the opportunity to do, which is to look at life from a different angle and actively choose God through your choices with regards to this book and working the program it contains.

On the surface, it doesn't sound like a tough thing to do, to complete the first three steps of this program, and honestly, even when reading about the fourth step it doesn't appear to be all that challenging. But when you look deeper into what it is you have accomplished by surrendering your life over to a power greater than yourself in step three, as well as setting the contextual stage for understanding the ego enough to be aware of the choices you were making in steps one and two, by the time you have reached step four, which requires a major undertaking to complete, you have already asked God, the creator and sustainer of the universe, the Alpha and Omega, the up and the down, the left and the right, the here and the there and everything in between, to remove the ownership of your life from your hands and have placed the direction of life forever more into the hands of Absolute Love. Not only have you given your will and life over to something greater than yourself, but you've taken time to deliberately look back on a life that up until recently you had seeming control over, but at the end of the day wasn't worth more than the possibility of what can come from letting go and letting God take the wheel. It is incredible what you have accomplished by simply buying or finding this book, reading the introduction and forward of the book, staying with the dialogue through steps four and winding up here at five. By finishing this step, you're making the conscious decision to look back over the totality of your life and write down what attachments came up needing to be let go of, and what that actually means is that you have chosen God and Truth and Love for your future over what the ego has in store for you.

You have chosen Life, my friends.

You have chosen Love, my friends.

What you have done up until this point through working these steps is nothing short of a miracle. One day soon, in the not-so-distant future, you will be able to take another person through these steps because you finished working them. By working these steps, you have chosen to be the change you wished to see in the world, and because of being that change first, you're now able to share the message of change with everyone you come in contact with by just having your presence available to people.

At some point in your life, you will be able to share your journey and experience with another person, and because of you working these steps you'll be able to pass this information on to the next journeyman looking for a little more peace and joy in their life. And because of that you'll be able to deliver God to them as well through a personal connection with divinity. You are the change the world needs and the change the world will need for generations to come – all because you let God know you're ready to be the change and decided to practice surrender, forgiveness and gratitude.

I am filled with joy you made it this far and have but a little more way to go to find completion with these steps. Hang in there, stay loose and focused, and don't forget to watch the world stay the same around you but yet different at the same time, all while the world notices that something has changed in you. The way it works is someone you know or people you meet will say there's something different about you, something engaging and peaceful, and because of this you won't have to proselytize about God, you'll be a witness of God's nature by just what you are, and then best of all, be able to point them in the direction of finding joy in their own life not through telling someone a half-truth, but by speaking from firsthand experience. You are learning how to fish while actively fishing. Soon, you won't catch someone a fish, but teach them how to string up a line. You are living a spiritual life by working these steps, and before you know it, the realization will arise that you made a decision to live like Jesus without ever knowing it. Because you live like Jesus means you have the opportunity to experience God for yourself in the days and weeks and months ahead. Living like Jesus is what this book is all about. This book is not about religion or buying into what a religion tells you – this book is about actively being love and producing love through righteous actions and deliberate devotion.

Mark my words: if you finish these steps integrously, earnestly, honestly, and whole heartedly, your life will have a noticeable change forever, and the world will take notice and comment about the fact that happiness is all around you, even in the face of difficult times and challenges. The world will take notice that you have changed before you ever notice the difference in how you move throughout life. Your family will notice there's something different about you, as will your friends and colleagues, before you notice you're moving through the world differently from ever before.

TRUTHS:

(The Gospel of Thomas) *Your salvation comes from being aware of what is already inside of you. If you are unaware, you will remain subject to death.*

(The Lankavatara Sutra) *One achieves self-realization by practicing mental concentration. He will thus come to the state of Noble Wisdom.*

(The Upanishads) *The purpose of things in your life is not for you to love them, but to love the Self in all things.*

(The Tao Te Ching) *He who identifies himself with the world, receives the world. He who sees himself as the world comes to accept it.*

CONTEMPLATING ON TRUTH:

I spent the better part of three decades thinking that

my salvation would be found outside of myself and in the hands of another. I spent more than thirty years looking for the answers to life's toughest questions from sources beyond the confines of my inner-being. I looked and I looked and I looked, until all the looking led me back to the source, and to the answer I had been pursuing for so many years: God is not to be found somewhere outside of me, but was within the very core of my being the entire time. This revelation brought not only comfort in my darkest hour but hope for the chance at a better life than I was currently experiencing. If God is found within me, God is found within you as well, and because God is found within you and me, God is at the core of all mankind for both the lost and the saved alike. The truth of existence, consciousness and the riddles of old, is not that we have anything to accomplish while in physicality, but we have only to recognize, experience, witness and observe that which is within all of us quietly presenting itself a million times over in every moment of now, which is why realization springs forth from being in this body to begin with. If you choose to remain unaware that within you is the source of all of life, then you are choosing to ignore the most precious gift we all have - the gift of Life. We are not separate from the Creator, we're one with the Creator. We're not outside of God's grace, but many are continually operating ignorantly to the fact that grace is a gift already given, just maybe not yet realized and not yet allowed to be received.

The fastest way to salvation is through humility and forgiveness, and consequently, the fastest way to understanding who Jesus was in the flesh, is through exercising humility and forgiveness in your own life repeatedly. Jesus was made flesh for a myriad of reasons, but one of those reasons is much more powerful than most people choose to see: What Jesus was, is also what you are in your core, total potential for a life lived through complete and total unconditional love for yourself, mankind, and the Creator, for you already are all of those things you just don't know that yet. What was in Jesus is also within you, it's just you haven't taken the time to look within and search deep enough for the truth yet. One cannot look within without noticing there's more than flesh and bones present around the heart.

The linear world is designed in such a way as to keep our attention focused outward on the goings on of everyday existence, as opposed to looking within for the truth found through self-realization as the result of deliberate devotion. All that we see around ourselves is a wide array of opportunities to play in the chaos or to choose to quiet such noise through inner contemplation and seek Peace within. The hardships that one faces in life are not due to being unequipped for the journey of life, but in believing that Life is found in what the eyes see, as opposed to what the experiencer experiences, the observer observes, and the witnesser witnesses. Pain in this life is the result of resisting life as it unfolds, whereas joy in this life comes from watching life unfold while surrendering over one's control over it and desire to change it, and experiencing self-realization as a result.

It is wise and good to love all that you are for the sake of loving what is, but it is wiser to love all that you are because you have concentrated long enough on what you are not, in order to see that Love is all you truly are – love, in a greater or lesser degree of intensity. Only through mental concentration, only through mindfulness, only through contemplation, meditation, forgiveness, surrender, prayer and the like, and all of that which quiets the endless chatter of thoughts within one's head, can someone realize that Noble Wisdom speaks louder than the fire of a thousand cannons, or the march of a million neatly filed soldiers approaching the lines of battle. Noble Wisdom can be had only when someone no longer is attracted to the sights and sounds of the masses, but instead has chosen to experience the truth of witnessing what arises externally but not reacting to it or fixating on an opinion of it.

At this point if you choose so, at the point of walking forward with self-realization as your unfolding, subjective life experience, one can finally know that the content of the outside world is of little consequence to the energies of fluctuating truth now flowing through your beingness upon placing no judgment on what's found within the outside world. Mental concentration for the spiritual seeker is but a milestone one reaches moving up the evolutionary scale of consciousness, however, for the person who just seeks happiness and joy in their current life, mental concentration is a wonderful place to start, because it leads to self-realization.

The way most people on earth view one another is as separate beings coexisting, and because of this common perception of life, one often overlooks the value of connecting with one's Self through a loving interaction with another. We are one another's mirrors, not one another's enemies. The way many people on earth look at Life, is as something meant to fulfill their wishes at little cost, and because of this garage-sale mentality, all the riches in the world will bring little Self-realization to any being, only more Saturday morning lawn sales without easy parking.

The way people see the world around them is based on its appearance to them and rooted in their current level of consciousness, i.e. how pretty a person is, how shiny an object is, how fashionable an idea might be, and so on, which is subjectively without objectivity, as well as based in the attracter pattern of glamour and not truth, whereas the true nature of the world around us is not how a thing appears but the absolute nature of essence in its many varieties of consciousness expressing itself within appearance and non-appearance simultaneously. The purpose of having "things" in our life is not so we can love them as we love that which is found within another, but so we may have an amplitude of ways to experience the true essence of that which we are beneath the glare, 'the Self in all things.' The content of the linear arises out of the context of the non-linear, or another way to understand this is: the stuff of life comes from Life itself. When we look at something on face value, especially as we seek to define its value, only what one holds as glamourous will amount to a gain, whereas, if one surrenders over their judgment of value to God, suddenly, what we once believed to be of great value now isn't, and what was once thought to be of little value now is. What one owns is not what a person is, and what a person experiences is not what one is, but something magical happens when a person lets go of their attachment of what they believe something to be in exchange for surrendering over their opinion to God. What one sees is no longer a limited definition rooted in benefit or cost, but a viewpoint of what resides within the essence of what one is looking at. When a person no longer sees loss or gain when gazing out into the world around them, but sees the value inherit to a person or thing because of the context from which it arises, that viewer is now moving closer to God with every step forward.

It's a difficult obstacle to step over when talking about being in the world but not of it, with the difficulty coming in the form of not knowing what the steps are to see yourself as the totality. We all have/had times of hardship, loneliness, desperation, solitude, depression, and every other form of occurrence and happenstance known as being part of man's experience. However, we've all experienced moments of love as well, moments of joy, times of beauty, friendship, bliss, and even exuberant moments of pure happiness and possibly ecstasy. When the seeker realizes they are none of these things, neither the high nor low points, but that which witnesses them, the seeker has the opportunity to approach acceptance for the lot of it all, and it is only through acceptance of the entirety can one begin to let go of that which no longer defines who they choose to be as the singular.

Once one has accepted they are one with the world and a part of everything in it, and not run by a world without choice, they begin to understand the world is the perfect place to be in order to get where they have the potential to go, while being in the world but not of it moving forward. Living one's life like a prayer is what being in the world but not of it means. Living one's life like a prayer is easier than most people realize. Being in the world but not of it, when broken down to a few choices, is the blueprint for seeing "himself as the world," and accepting it:

1. Forgive everyone for everything.

2. Surrender over everything all the time.

3. Allow gratitude and thankfulness to become part of conscious praise for the Creator and what's created.

If you choose to identify with the world, you'll be subject to the whims of the personal ego and the direct illusions of the will of the masses. On the other side of the coin, if you choose to see yourself as in the world but not of it, the momentary times of joy, happiness, sadness, loneliness, etc. will just be experienced as stimuli worth acknowledging and surrendering over. The truth is, you, reading this now, are not what you think you are. You are not disconnected from the source. You are not alone in this journey towards wholeness. And you are not on this planet to be better than anyone else with regards to comparison's sake. You are here to realize all of these things are needed so that acceptance can springboard your life into one characterized by courage and grateful living.

INSTRUCTIONS FOR STEP FIVE:

The person doing the steps finds someone to share with what they found within step 4. This person should be trusted, if possible have completed the steps before them, and is meant to be a sounding board for listening to what was found, not as someone to make you feel better about what was found. This step is not therapy or even counseling. The person who listens takes notes about aspects of what they hear as themes or as aspects of what continues to be repeated throughout the conversation. Once the person sharing their step four work is finished, the person listening simply remarks on what notes were taken and what inspiration came to mind for them as they listened.

It is best for this step to be taken in one sitting together, with breaks taken as necessary. This step can also be taken over the phone or via a facetime feature. The purpose for someone listening is to lend their life experience to what they hear, and this step is as much about the listener as it is about the speaker.

The listener listens until the speaker is done speaking. All information shared within their time together is confidential and between the two parties and God. The time spent together should be away from prying ears and is best done in seclusion somewhere with proper ventilation and within proximity to bathrooms and ample fluids.

Once the listener has shared their notes with the speaker, the listener can feel free to give their notes to the now finished 5th stepper.

STEP FIVE

-

I admitted to God, myself, and to another human being, the exact nature of my findings.

STEP FIVE PRAYER

-

Thank you Lord for the gift of honesty, the gifts of love, and for the opportunity today to share with you and someone else in the blessings of truth.

Chapter 6

EXPERIENCING NEUTRALITY

I was more than ready...

If you take time to look up the definition of the word neutrality in the dictionary, it doesn't do a good enough job synopsizing it for the purpose of this book. So, for this chapter and the conversation ahead, we'll put forth our own definition for neutrality in the sense of providing a spiritually based context. Neutrality: the state of being neither for something nor against something, taking no sides; the action of being fine with however the chips fall, not sweating the small stuff; acceptance of life on life's terms; not demanding of a particular outcome.

The first time I looked at the levels of consciousness, I was struck by the fact that courage was used as the definer for entering the positive emotional sets of life, and that neutrality was seen as a higher level of consciousness than courage. However, once I gave the two words more thought and spent more time learning about the definitions of each, the meanings of each and the context of each, I was able to see the perfect nature of courage coming before neutrality, and neutrality being a higher level of calibrated consciousness than courage.

As we spent time looking at the lower attracter fields and lesser levels of consciousness from apathy and grief to anger and pride, along with everything in-between, we were able to paint a picture of someone falling in these places of wanting as also being a slave to the ego. When someone finds themselves calibrating below the level of courage, their life is not their own because their life is run by the base levels of one's animal nature, where the animal is out for survival at any cost, regardless of the fact that as humans we no longer have to kill another animal to get what we want. The ego works for survival, and because of this fact, when you're under the level of courage, you believe you're the thing always wanting more, and rarely does this person ever see that in fact they're not the thing wanting more but actually something else, currently unaware that they're more than the thing always fighting for survival and winning at all costs. Through courage to surrender the lesser for the unknown greater, someone surrounded by fear has the innate ability to transcend the illusion that fear is a hurdle too high to jump over. Courage is what the soldier has to embody to stand up and walk through the hail of bullets. Courage is what the battered wife has to embody in order to stand up to her abuser and choose life over bondage. It takes courage to ever reach a point where one has the choice to be okay with life how it is, because without courage there is no opportunity to see any outcome in the short-term still leads in a direction worth pursuing. Without the gift of courage, and without the fact that courage isn't something you can fake but something you have to choose based on faith, it makes perfect sense as to why one has to first show signs of courage in order to reach a point in life where they can be satisfied with whatever elements are the outcomes of future decisions.

An interesting aspect of the calibrated levels of consciousness which I have now studied and put into practice daily for many years, is that the vast majority of American pastors within the faith of Christianity calibrate in the fluctuating levels of courage. It's important to note, no particular level from courage to enlightenment is any better than another level, it's just simply where one finds themselves in order to move towards yet another level at another time, likened to building blocks. In the same vein as many pastors in the United States, within the evangelical church, their style of praise and worship and the method they employ for grand displays of modern music pumped forth by smiling faces and large speakers, usually calibrates two to three ticks higher on the scale in the realms of willingness and acceptance, which is precisely why someone entering a church service feeling down in the dumps can have such an uplifting experience within the service but come crashing back down once they leave. At these levels of willingness and acceptance, which we'll dive into deeper through the next couple of steps, we see that from courage to neutrality, and from neutrality to willingness and even acceptance, monumental leaps in one's level of consciousness are taking place. Meaning, the love present at the level of willingness or acceptance is far superior to the amount of love felt all around someone who finds their life characterized by courage. Courage is faith in action whereas neutrality is more defined as faith in glad tidings. The reason I bring this all up is to show that as one progresses through the steps and finds more and more love present as a conclusion, just like attending a church service you find more upliftment through a loud band rocking out as opposed to the message of many pastors, is the same for levels of consciousness – the higher one travels the more innate joy one experiences.

Neutrality as a way of life is a blessed situation to find oneself in, and without the courage needed to surrender the lesser over to the greater, all without any proof that life will be better because of it, one would never have the opportunity to feel okay about life taking on whatever shape it takes on. With neutrality, one becomes okay if an endeavor works out and okay if it doesn't, fine with getting a new job and still fine with the one they have, all while allowing for the chance to start anew and feeling confident if all stays the same. Neutrality is a powerful level to calibrate at, and just like what will come in step 6, and the meaning for doing it, one is okay with further surrendering their life to God because at this point what do they have to lose?

Neutrality is characterized through the descriptors in Hawkins's map of consciousness by having a view of God where the Creator appears to be enabling change for the better. At this level, life is satisfactory at worst and approaching hopeful at best. The emotional state which best describes how they approach the world is one of natural trust in life and trust in their potential, unlike in anger where trust is virtually nonexistent. And finally, their process for examining life is one of release and letting go of past grudges and attachments to future possibilities. Very few religious leaders of a congregation calibrate at the level of neutrality, with the best of them surrendering over their service to the Holy Spirit so that the pastor might take a back seat so that Love can come through him or her for the time their flock is present.

If there are any pastors reading this material, I have a few pieces of advice for you, and you can take it or leave it: 1) never stop surrendering your life and your fears over to God; 2) always be honest with your congregation about your fears and the limits of your experiences with God and with your faith; 3) put away the notes, speak from personal experience, and surrender over the pulpit every time for the Holy Spirit to deliver the sermon.

For all of you reading this who attend a religious service throughout the week, if your leader doesn't do these three things, pray for him/her to do so, and ask God to provide your congregation's figurehead with the humility to speak from their current level of knowingness about God and not from a place where they talk about things they've heard others say about another's experience with being alive and with experiencing Love. The greatest message a pastor has is the one they didn't write, the one that comes from the heart and is based on their life with God. If your pastor doesn't do this, or they tell you how you should live through fearful words as opposed to personal actions which produce fruit in their life, find another place to worship and a new house to call your community, or else risk your own divine connection with God dwindling as the byproduct.

TRUTHS:

(Chuang Tzu) *The wise man moves about, not caring about home or possessions. He lives simply. His feet leave no footprints. Thus, the perfect person is one whose vessel is empty.*

(The Gospel of Thomas) *There was a wealthy man who said to himself, "I should fill my storehouses with grain, and then I will be secure." This was his intention, but that very night he died.*

(The Dhammapada) *There are two paths: one is directed towards wealth, the other towards freedom. The monk who understands this renounces world desires.*

(The Bhagavad Gita) *With a heart unattached to the outer world, those who seek Me find joy and happiness.*

CONTEMPLATING ON TRUTH:

The days of my childhood can be described as running about from here to there without purpose or intent, with only new experience as the basis for movement. The days of my teenage years were still spent running about from here to there, but my life took on some intent for the first time, and it was because of this intent I had a framework to base my choices upon, and a solid direction to move my body towards. As I found myself moving into my young adult years, the framework which served me so well previously, was replaced by a flimsier version of movement based upon controlled chaos, which had purpose, but with which its intent was no longer to produce the fruits of righteous action, but the withering of vines found within a garden neglected. As my adult years carried on in the same fashion as the farmer who has lost his will to properly tend to his crops, I was prematurely dying on the vine.

Somewhere between childhood and adulthood, I started caring about possessions, and living had gone from one of simplicity to one of simply existing. My feet left their prints in every direction I traveled as my adult years waned on, and there was scant a place that was tread without the ability for the world to take notice that I was losing my footing. My vessel was full of the distractions of life, full of disappointments from life, full of addictions to lesser forms of life, full of wants and desires about happiness returning to my life in the form of a lighter heart and a softer brow, but in the end, it took my feet almost walking off the cliff in order to realize that the lightest and most fruitful load a man can carry is that of an empty vessel.

It was surrendering over my intent in the moment and letting go of my attachment to the life that I was currently living, which enabled me to finally be able to become free from fear in all its forms. And today, in this moment, the thought of deliberately leaving my print on this world no longer matters much, for it either will or it won't happen, but it definitely won't be because I forced it upon the history books. The gift of neutrality is this: either something will happen, or it won't, either way "I'm cool." Neutrality, a raise in consciousness from courage, holds a tremendous amount of power within it. To be good with any outcome of an endeavor is the first true sign that happiness as a subjective reality is setting in and coming to dominate.

We all come into this life at a time predetermined and chosen, chosen not only by a creator but also by the creation. Once born, what is left up to us is not to know when we will die, but how we choose to live once we are incarnated again into this particular physicality. We are given the gift of choice in this lifetime, the choice to be or not to be, and that is not only the question but ultimately the answer. It is because of this gift that one can choose to live each day like it's their last, which helps grow the possibilities of today. In direct opposition to living this way is living like every day will be followed by yet another one identical to it, which can lead a person to believe there's more time for salvation and evolution than what's present now. We came into this life on a particular day and we will leave it on a particular day, but the time in-between is why we are here, for it is the space in-between the goal posts that one plays the game, with either goal post only representing what the boundaries of the playing field are.

Planning for your future self is a worthy and noble endeavor, but not at the cost of losing sight that this moment is the only gift of certainty that one has in life. When we store up riches for the future and we choose not to share with the world that which we possess in the current, we run the risk of entering the next world without the grain-house of the soul properly stockpiled. There is a fine balance between preparing for old age and truly living while you're on your way there, and I have threaded that needle very closely at times, but the secret to keeping both halves within balance, and the truth of the matter for myself, both sides of the coin (life & death) are equally important as long as the owner of this precious metal has no attachment to which way the coin flip goes.

Do we want to be on death's bed wishing we had done more for people, or do we want to rest peacefully as we slip into the next chapter certain that we left the world a better place than we found it? This is not your first lifetime. This is not your first rodeo. This will not be the last time you do the dance of life. Some of you, however, have found a savior, and some of you will find enlightenment, others will find happiness, joy, peace and even prosperity, but the flipside of storing your riches on earth as opposed to in heaven, is that you'll miss out experiencing heaven on earth as well.

There was a time in my life when I was consumed with what the world appeared to be able to provide me, namely in the form of happiness through acquisition. Whether it be the allure of fancy cars, large homes, expensive dinners, nights out on the town, a particular type of romantic partner, and whatever else promised external relief from having to look within myself for answers to continued unhappiness. I remember the day I departed from that path and set sail towards the great unknown world of what God had in store for my daily goings on, and for the unknown land of happiness found within as opposed to the hope of momentary dopamine hits found through another purchase. It was through surrendering over my wants and desires on a moment-to-moment basis for a prolonged period of time, before there was any empty space to begin pointing towards a path of finding my heart affixed close to that which created me. It was as though I had allowed the pursuit of glamour to build a wall around my inner being, cutting it off completely from what some refer to as, "the sunlight of the spirit."

However, today, I know beyond a shadow of a doubt, pursuing the world left me full of emptiness. But living as a monk would, with regards to letting go of desires, wants, attachments and expectations, I somehow found what I had been searching for from all the shiny objects outside of me for so long – happiness. You see, happiness is not a reality only for the special few, it's a choice for anyone who stops living for themselves and starts asking a basic question of the world around them: where can I be of service? The truth is, wealth is not a good nor bad thing, and freedom is not better than modern day indentured servitude to base desires, because they're both subjective realities that lead inevitably towards the same realization: there's more to this life than meets the eye. I could not have experienced freedom without first chasing after the trappings of the shiny world around me, only to come up internally empty from the pursuit. The beautiful thing about pursuing freedom as opposed to chasing after wealth is that a byproduct of experiencing freedom as your reality can also lead to immense wealth as a result. However, when one chooses to put the pursuit of wealth above their pursuit of serving God, freedom never follows, only spiritual slavery. If you desire happiness, pursue freedom over wealth, and wealth will either come or won't come as a result but not because you did anything to get it.

In case you have not figured it out yet, surrender is

the key to finding joy and happiness in your everyday life. When I stop and focus back on all of the time wasted in this lifetime and others where I spent my waking hours attached to what others thought of me or fretted about what would happen "if" or "if only," I am brought back to this moment of right now, this very second, where the me of today can barely recognize the life I lived yesterday. I chose to pursue a connection with God over an attachment to the outer world, in what many would perceive as an aggressive pursuit, but in all reality, what I did at the basest level was constantly and consistently surrender everything over to my Creator until there was nothing left of the old Mason to hang a hat on. What happens through deep surrender is life gets re-contextualized, and new choice matrixes begin presenting themselves as viable choice hierarchies, and those new streams of choice create a new foundation for living life.

Today, I am rebuilt on a foundation of connectedness to the source, and life looks nothing like it did at earlier points in this body. Today, synchronicity guides movement, and today, a true communion with the higher self is what shines through from moment to moment. The key to un-attaching from the outside world is first realizing one is not of this world to start with, but wholly and better still, holy just visiting.

Step two towards un-attachment requires letting go of wants, desires, expectations and attachments to what one believes defines who one is in the world at large. The third step towards finding joy and happiness in everyday life is being able to recognize these gifts in real time once they arrive. The last obvious point of life that many would consider a secret, which I will share now, is that happiness is a choice, and just as much of a choice as sorrow, but it takes consistently surrendering the ego structure in order to witness life from a place of having a "heart unattached to the outer world." Having a heart unattached to the outer world doesn't mean the world will disappear from view, or that you'll be fired from your job, or that you'll vanish into a mindset of "nothing matters." Being unattached to the outer world simply opens up room in your day-to-day life where natural states of experiencing God have room to seep through the cracks forming within the personal ego structure. If you desire happiness and joy as regular subjective experiences, stop wanting anything, forgive everyone all the time, and surrender over every thought to God.

INSTRUCTIONS FOR STEP SIX:

This is one of the quickest steps we have in the program for transcending the ego and fear in all of its forms. This step sets up a second part found within step seven, which is also mutually as quick but quite a bit loftier in its attempt. For this step, find a quiet place to read the step and the prayer internally. Once you have taken a few minutes to meditate and pray on what this step and the prayer says, read out loud as declarative sentences the step and the prayer. If you don't mean this step or don't have time for this prayer, put the information away and come back to it.

STEP SIX

-

I am entirely ready to have God remove my attachments to the baggage of life found through steps 4 and 5.

STEP SIX PRAYER

-

I am ready for your help oh Lord, and for you to take the things that brought shame and destruction into my life away from who I am moving forward.

Chapter 7

EXPERIENCING WILLINGNESS

Humility was the key...

Step seven is a bigtime step in this program, not saying the rest of the steps aren't important or immensely valuable to work through, but if you've reached this phase of the program it means you've worked through the steps it takes to get here. You have arrived at a point where you can look back at your time of surrendering and moving into forgiveness, where seeing your life for what it once was and for what it is now, has moved you one step closer to the opportunity for moving into what it can be.

In step seven, we ask God to remove from our life the burdens of past mistakes, past judgments, character defects, pains, resentments, angers, frustrations, and all other aspects of the ego that we once believed to be what we are. We're not just asking God to do something with these things from our psyche, we're asking God to remove the residue of them from ever being in attendance as a belief system about how we would have described to the world and to ourselves the exact nature of our life.

In steps one through three, we worked a three-fold angle of surrender into the mix where we realized we needed help, came to believe that we couldn't do it on our own, and then finally asked God for help with something that left to our own devices would have only persisted ad infinitum. In steps four and five, we looked back over our life and put down on paper what we found. We then took what we found and cycled it all through a different lens of examining the past. Once we took a full inventory of past moments in time worth surrendering over, we shared what we found with our self, God, and another human, so as to speak out loud what we once kept internally so tight as who we believed ourselves to be. Moreover, once taking these steps and arriving at this chapter and inevitably step seven, what proceeded immediately this step was once again becoming ready and priming our mind for the next big leap of faith, which we will be presented here at the end of all our dialogue.

For close to a decade, from the age of about twenty or so to about thirty-two, what characterizes willingness as a level of consciousness is what I pretended be for the world to see. I pretended to be motivational, aspirational, thankful, and humble. I was doing my best to fake the magic that comes from a life of helping others, while doing my best internally to find my own prosperity out of it. I held onto judgments about life, anger over not being where I thought I deserved to be in life, resentments of others for getting what I wanted before me, and always close by was the hope that someone else would come into my life and make it all better.

Willingness as a level of consciousness means a whole lot more than the basic definition of this word as defined by dictionary.com as "consent or readiness to do something." When we look at willingness as a level of consciousness, what we find is that willingness means to have the ability to help someone move on to greater and better things by just the presence of your intent for them, because that's what works for you. You're just sharing what you are because it works for you innately. When you don't need anything, it is easier to help someone else find what they are looking for. Think Tony Robbins in his prime, or place any other public speaker or motivator in his place, and you'll know what willingness represents in a lifeform. Beyond the ability to be all motivation at this phase of one's evolution towards God, willingness also means the person occupying this level has the innate ability to strive towards greater things for not only themselves but for larger groups of people as well. Some of the greatest CEOs and public servants we have calibrate in or around willingness. This level of life is also the first time that by just being you, the ability to bring together what's needed to create change on a larger scale is present and accounted for. The energy of this level moves out before your every step and has a way of seamlessly delivering whatever's needed in front of you as it's needed for whatever comes next. This stage of evolving towards Love is accomplishable for anyone working these steps and is not at all an impossible place to get to. If you have followed the steps up until now, continue to work the steps from this point forward, forgive yourself and everyone else in the world for everything that comes your way, and fully embrace gratitude as a way of life, and you will at the very least end up as someone who embodies willingness as your level of moving throughout life.

At this level, we also see the altruistic side of life become self-evident where someone feels called to be a police officer, fire fighter, EMT, teacher or excellent life-coach. Willingness is characterized by having the ability to put the needs of others above your own, in both scope and magnitude, and done so in large part because for the first time in life, you realize that there is no such thing as scarcity, and that by giving another what they need, you're actually helping yourself be more successful. At this level, there is almost nothing you can't accomplish by focusing your intent on something to get it accomplished.

All that I just described was what I pretended to be and what I wanted the world to think I was. For fits and starts, I was aspects of this level of consciousness even when I found myself in hell, but I wasn't this level of consciousness in reality which is very far from any aspects of hell. Like what was stated in the previous chapter, if something calibrates at this frequency or above it, the energy coming forth has the ability to lift someone out of despair, feelings of anguish, and from overall states of depression if they find themselves within its presence. Like a church's praise and worship time, the energy of this atmosphere is what lifts someone up, not the words within the songs or even the notes within the music, it's the entirety of the moment and the intent of the moment that creates a healing and uplifting atmosphere. More people attend non-denominational churches in the U.S. because of their praise and worship time and how it makes them feel, not because of the person doing the preaching.

Not all motivators or company leaders lead from a place of such magnitude, but the ones who truly calibrate at these levels are no doubt the same people others choose to emulate through weekend retreats designed to teach leadership, and leadership books written about important motivators throughout time. A coach who comes from this place of love is able to transform a team who lost more than they won last year into winners this year, but not through strategy and the x's and o's, but through being the change the team needed to stop playing for themselves and start playing for the sake of the team's success. If you find a life-coach who resonates at this level, not only are they problem-solvers at heart, but they truly believe in your potential based on what they know their own potential to be.

Another beautiful thing about calibrating at this level is for the first time it truly feels like something is guiding you. At this level, any accomplishment is possible, including either using your power to accumulate wealth or using your power to bring wealth to an entire nation. The best leaders from around the world have a shared level of consciousness in and around willingness.

TRUTHS:

(The Chandogya Upanishad) *Things of the world are transitory. If one dies without first having realized the Self, there is no happiness here, or hereafter.*

(The Tao Te Ching) *As fresh as morning breeze, feeling reborn, I wander here and there without a care in the world. Let others chase after wealth. I am content with the gifts provided by Mother Tao.*

(The Gospel of Mark) *Go and sell what you have, and give the money to the poor. Then you will have riches in heaven.*

(The Dhammapada) *If you wish to be free from old age and rebirth, become an island unto yourself, and eliminate all your imperfections.*

CONTEMPLATING ON TRUTH:

Realizing the Self looks different in different religions. Realizing the Self is experienced by many as hearing about God, or Jesus, or Krishna, or the Buddha, or Allah, or whatever name one holds onto in their part of the world. However, the subjective realization of the Self has nothing to do with religion or names, titles, or any other definable separator contained within a religious text. If one continually searches for the Self within, they will find it, but if one searches for the Self outside of their inner being, they'll have to settle for only shared definitions within religious pursuits, mostly defined by others' experiences of God, and maybe, just maybe, have a moment or two in their life when reality defies rational explanation.

I spent the majority of my life looking for happiness

119

from the world around me, or from the love of a person who happened to be in my life romantically, only to continue that search for completion long after the final farewell cannon was fired on my relationship, or when the new car smell wore off the upholstery. The illusory moment of realization hit me when I found the happiest I had been in many years was not when I had the most amount of money, a girlfriend to call my love, new and fashionable clothes, or the latest designer sunglasses. No, happiness filled my being because my attachment to those things was leaving me, and what was replacing these transitory artifices of the world was a willingness to trust in that which created me, and more precisely, to trust that whatever created me would also provide all I need, all the time, which includes happiness. Once this truth was stumbled upon and the clouds parted from my previous view of what happiness meant to me, I began to realize that the Self, had always been there and will never leave, because we are one, forever and ever amen.

The good news is, God, the Self, the Holy Spirit, it's all the same thing in different aspects, and because the awareness of this fact is apparent within this current reality of life, it's present in your life even if you have never looked for it. God is always present and always everything at once. Until you see that, or choose to not judge that, you're only playing with your religion's understanding of God, which is very different from actually experiencing God. Understanding trumps ignorance, but experience trumps understanding every time.

Growing older, when compared to youth, has its advantages and disadvantages. With age comes wisdom but with youth comes energy. With age comes experience but with youth comes first-times. The list for both ends of the age spectrum can go on and on, however, both being older and younger carry along with them something in common worth noting: differing context. As a young man, I chased wealth because the world said I should. I chased financial prosperity because my ego said I should. I was reckless with love, ignorant of faith, repugnant towards advice, and downright hostile towards the gifts of Mother Tao. As a youth, I knew what the world was and I knew what I wanted from it, even though looking back I can see how clueless I was for many years.

Today, I have a different context of understanding with regards to life than even a decade ago; one built on the same foundation of chasing after something. However, today, what the world and the ego says is valuable, holds no sway over me, and without chasing after the world as a prime directive these days, I am left with the experiences of contentment and prosperity as primary operating mechanisms. The context of existence today has changed from yesteryear, despite the sins of my past once being so prominent. Today, through a contemplative lifestyle and dedication to truth, what has become clear to me is that chasing after wealth creates circles, while being content with what one is has a magical way of drawing straight lines from one perfect moment to the next perfect moment. As the morning breeze of fresh perspective runs across my face today, I am now continually reborn with the promise of what every new day could have in store, and I wander from room to room without a care in the world, and all because I let others chase after acquisition while I chase after God instead. In the context of life today, I see lasting happiness is an option for anyone and at the same time cannot be paid for, but minor moments of excited surprise can, and conversely, the pursuit of pleasure for pleasure's sake never leads a man directly to Mother Tao, but towards something far less enjoyable in the long run. It's simple, you cannot serve two masters with equal vigor, so either the world is your king, or pursuing truth is what rules the roost.

For years, I gathered bits and pieces of clothing from all over the world. If someone was to ask me what my personal style was, I'm not sure I could have answered the question and it would have taken some consideration. I had everything from tailored suits and wingtips, vans and cutoff jean shorts to khakis and polos. I had athletic shoes that totaled over 15 in count, and I had hats far too many to ever wear, most of which weren't worn more than once. I collected fragments of styles along my life and created a hodgepodge of fashion, but most days I could be found in a white, V-neck t-shirt, Levi's jeans and an old pair of Chuck's. Then, out of nowhere, I was called to a life of service and tight space, and I had to get rid of everything I spent years collecting, including clothes, but also everything else a person collects to live in this world. At first, I was planning to sell it all and put the money towards a chosen endeavor, but then, the Holy Spirit instructed me to give everything away free of payment. As it all unfolded in the beginning, I wasn't sure why I was supposed to give it all away, but I eventually listened to the inner knowingness and dispersed what I owned far and wide; the result of which has been life-transforming. From listening to the message that filled my heart and then living out that message with action, heaven suddenly was made clear to me in an experienceable way, and the rest as they say is history.

The beautiful thing about life is, God never forces anyone to do anything, but when you listen to the sometimes off-beat requests made by the Creator, heaven becomes an everyday experience. Unbeknownst to me at the time of freely parting with a life's worth of stuff, I was being groomed to see how far I was willing to listen to the spirit of God speaking internally within my being. As time crept along over the next several years, it wasn't just clothing I was asked to give away, but every dollar in my possession, and every dollar more than once, more than twice, more than three times, and at the point of writing this here, I have been beyond broke more than four times since listening to God about being of service through giving away earthy possessions. The truth is, one needs not things to be happy, nor obvious choices for dinner to be fed. From firsthand experience I can relate, when you give away what you think makes you you, one finds out you're anything but you.

A man can spend his entire life working to rid himself of his imperfections only to realize just after physical death, there were no imperfections to let go of, only choices worth surrendering over and not worth repeating another time. The root of imperfection is not imperfection, but infinite love. All content is based upon, and arises out of, an ultimate and absolute context, which is why imperfection is not based on its opposite or its likeness, but on that which created "choice" to begin with, because without choice one could never choose differently next time. Seeing imperfection is entirely based upon ones' own perspective at the time of the choice, and ones' perspective is entirely based upon ones' consciousness level, and ones' consciousness level is based upon a myriad of factors, none of which being imperfect, but more precisely, misguided and naïve at the time.

If you desire to reach enlightenment as a goal for this life or the next and/or move towards the light more than towards the dark, or to see the world as Christ did, or just make it through a day without cursing your brother, becoming an island unto yourself is a way to accomplish these goals. So, what does it mean to become an island unto yourself? Quite simply, it means to live your life like a prayer, while simultaneously surrendering over any fear to God that arises in the ever-persistent moment of now. This may sound like a lot of work or even total nonsense, but in truth, it's not work or nonsense at all, only conscious decision making fueled by loving intent. One can be an island unto themselves and thereby free of old age and rebirth, when daily surrender leads the island builder into a consciousness level of transcendence over the direction and pull of the ego. We don't rid ourselves of imperfections by neglecting or walking past them, but by seeing them for what they are, waves against the shore and nothing more. The island is the context, but until one learns how to move throughout the day in a surrendered fashion, the content of daily choices one may have while on an island, like chopping down coconuts, taking walks on a beach, watching sunsets and sunrises, these will be seen only as aspects of life repeating itself while leading towards old age and death, and not as aspects of life that help one transcend having to choose old age and death again next time.

INSTRUCTIONS FOR STEP SEVEN:

As the next step that follows six, we take the same approach with this one. We find a quiet place secluded from the noise of the outside world, and we read the step and the prayer that goes along with it internally first. Once we are ready to take the step to completion, we say the step out loud and repeat the prayer as well, both in earnest and with faith applied. Once you have taken this step you are now ready to move into the last two aspects of this program which fall under the banners of forgiveness and gratitude. In this step, the person taking it is all that's needed to make it happen. Once completing this step by saying out loud what you have already said internally, put fifteen minutes on a timer and think about all that has taken place during your time with these steps so far.

STEP SEVEN

-

Lord, please remove from my life the scars of the past, all of my attachments to what I once believed myself to be, allow me to see you more clearly moving forward, and provide me the grace to forgive myself, you, and the world for where I once felt I was wronged.

STEP SEVEN PRAYER

-

Thank you for the gift of surrender, the blessing of forgiveness, and for the promise of gratitude to come as a way of life. I love you - thank you for loving me more than I love myself.

Chapter 8

EXPERIENCING ACCEPTANCE
I became willing...

The level of acceptance, as well as step eight, from a certain vantage point, both share equal properties. To be coming from a place of acceptance means to allow what is to remain what is, left unchanged and without effort on your part to create a different way. Meaning, life is actually seen as a gift that is continually unfolding, ever evolving, in constant creation, without end in sight for the soul. With acceptance for the person who inhabits this level of consciousness, life is no longer about wanting to change anything, but more about allowing for everything to be what it is without judgment. This is a high level of consciousness and one that brings about rapid change in one's surroundings by merely looking at something with directed intent.

Intent is something we have not spoken on much throughout this book, but it's worth focusing on here before moving on. There are any number of new-age, pseudo gurus and social media motivators who have bought the lie that the law of attraction is life changing or that the letter of that law is where some life-hack is found. In all reality, if one finds themselves at the level of acceptance, what they are is volumes more powerful than the little bit of truth that is found within the idea that all someone has to do to be rich is desire and visualize being rich. Acceptance is where the cancer patient reaches a point where getting better is fine with them or letting their body expire is fine as well, because either way their life is complete and not worth holding onto any longer out of fear for what comes next. Intent, especially at this level and within this step, is what drives change to move at a rate much faster than below this level. Through this step and this level of consciousness, one's intent can dictate the way life moves around them and for them. The key to intent is choosing and defining it, and the key to this step is doing it even though you are afraid that by making an amends to someone you'll somehow be hurting yourself in the process. Intent is part of how the spiritual aspirant moves from one level of consciousness to higher ones. Setting one's intent on reaching God recontextualizes your entire life and all of the choices you'll be presented with from here on out, unless you set your intent in another direction and have lesser choices pursued as realities. Intent is the way that choice is shuffled around to be presented with different options from another time in your life. If you find yourself at the level of acceptance, one's intent determines how life will react to you moving forward, because at this level of conscious evolution, compared to past lower levels, one has more power and love present in their being than at any point while in physicality. There is a sufficient amount of power within inhabiting acceptance where what you are draws in rapidly what's needed to continue defining to the world that in fact what you are is able to affect change through active inaction. At acceptance, active inaction is more powerful than simply action, and for the first time at this level one sees the truth in this statement. Through aiming one's intent in a particular direction, it's as if you're saying to the universe, this is what life is now about, and then life moves around to make it what your life is all about.

At acceptance through intent, your business, your family, your friends, your community, and your entire life starts becoming full of blessings, not because you're making blessings happen, but because what you are is now able to recognize that blessings take place all day without you having to do anything for them to be present. At this level everything feels easy, and whatever effort you put forth to achieve a goal is always the right amount of energy to achieve such goals. Likewise, with this step, just putting together the list of people, places, things and institutions where amends need to be made, brings about the choice to go and make the amends. This step is one of intent, and with that intent along with your list for the amends process, naturally what will arise are the opportunities needed to go make the amends process complete in the next step.

You'll notice in the wording of the step when you get to that point, it says "willing to make an amends," not will make an amends. The act of being willing is what sets up the level of acceptance as being present. Are you willing to make an amends to the people you harmed throughout your time on this earth, doing so only in the instances where you would not be harming yourself or another in the process? If the answer is yes, then you're closer to a level of acceptance than you realize. In the next step we become accepting of the fact that making an amends is what propels us forward towards transcending the ego and fear in all of its forms. This step, however, brings a person face-to-face with the world of acceptance, and we have to be willing to do something that takes faith before we can do the thing that cements faith as an action step.

Based on what Dr. Hawkins says about acceptance, when one reaches this level, their view of God is naturally one of seeing the creator as merciful, and likewise, their view of life is harmonious, as if everything just has a way of working out for the best. The emotional set they inhabit at their core is forgiveness, and the process by which their life is guided is one of transcendence. The previous sentence accounts for where we are in this program, and where this program has delivered the participant.

Prior to this step, we asked God to forgive us for the

choices we have made, and to remove the desire to continue making those choices again moving forward. This step is about accepting the forgiveness from God and being willing to have faith that through the amends process we'll come into contact with the reality of acceptance. Even though this step is not characterized by any outward action the world could notice, it's characterized by the inner action of acceptance, which is propelled through the intent of this program, which in turn is creating the habits needed to move forward in your life living in a truly spiritual manner. This step is acceptance, it is the action of inaction, and it is precisely what's needed to continue walking through fear no matter what.

By this point in the program, you are becoming the change in the world you once wished to see in it. You are becoming the light of the world, the friend on the other end of the phone, the blessing in another's life, and the presence of joy that will help another find their way out of the darkness. At this point in the program, you are putting into practice the love of God and simultaneously walking in the footsteps of Jesus, which maybe up until now you weren't aware you were doing. The way you're like Jesus is that you're not putting anything in between you and God, not your ego, not fear, nor a desire to hide any longer. No, you're willing to have faith in making things right with others because God has made things whole with you.

Acceptance is what will allow you to make an amends without desiring a particular outcome. Set your intent here and now by repeating these words out loud: *my intent is to be full of love and to see God for myself, as well as walk through the fear of making an amends to another person who might judge me for it – I surrender over the fear of practicing forgiveness, and I choose to walk straight ahead through whatever bullets come my way while chasing after God.*

Now that we have a basic idea about this step and the level of acceptance that corresponds with it, we can look a little deeper into what truth has to share with us from the great ones who walked before us.

TRUTHS:

(The Dhammapada) *As long as there is even the slightest desire on the part of a man for a woman, the mind is still imprisoned.*

(The Santiparva Mahabharata) *The wise man ceases seeking worldly pleasures. Thus, he reaches the highest goal.*

(The Tao Te Ching) *If our inner eye were to suddenly open, lust and greed would cease to exist.*

(The Book of Thomas the Contender) *Lust keeps humanity in bondage as long as people seek after those things that change and pass away.*

CONTEMPLATING ON TRUTH:

For many years, I pursued relationships out of a need to have completion in my life and validation in the mirror. I believed, by loving someone and having their love in return, I would finally become whole. I bought into the Hollywood storyline of finding love for myself through the direct love and romance found within the confines of a romantic relationship. I spent days, weeks, months, years, and every other measurement of time we have at our disposal, searching for Ms. Right, only to realize there's no such thing. The concept of "Ms. Right" and "Mr. Right" is mostly a myth. Both stories are fun to tell ourselves, and the promise that romantic love presents our fullest narrative for living is anything but boring. However, the problem isn't with engaging in the Hollywood promise of "foreverdom." It's in believing that someone else other than yourself is what will complete you. We're all complete the way we are, but all too often I failed to realize this because I failed to investigate who I truly was. We're not complete because we think we are, we're complete once we know what we are.

When I finally understood what completeness meant, and the sponsor of completeness is also the sponsor of creation, I suddenly realized, what I had been searching after for so long in another was me. Today, unlike in days past, I don't look to the world for happiness, satisfaction, completion, contentment, joy, prosperity, or whatever sounds fun in the moment. Now, I have the knowingness that without connecting with that which created me as my basis for completion, true love will only remain on the silver screen. My eyes no longer embrace desire as an option, nor do they see lust as a worthy choice. My mind no longer entertains thoughts of neediness, unyielding physical attraction, sexual demonstrations, or other animalistic displays of yearning. I embrace a connection when it's present and feel grateful for having had the opportunity for physical intimacy. Nothing outside of a person spawns happiness, and certainly not through romance as the doorway. Today, I see desire as a choice and no longer a circumstance. Today, the world is not what beckons me home, because today I am in the world but not of it. If one chooses rapturous desire, they experience enslavement, but if they choose surrender, freedom follows in short order. To be enslaved or not to be enslaved, that is the question.

When the spiritual traveler reaches a level of knowingness where his cares and concerns no longer deal with the physical world of wantingness, but instead have shifted to the inner-non-linear world as the basis of finding success, he will have started inching closer to the highest goal – the end goal being the peace that passes all understanding. To move past wants, desires, hopes, ambitions, motivations, cravingness, expectations and attachments, the highest goal becomes visible in the distance – the end goal of being in a state not fully explainable through language. There was a time when all of the worldly attachments above fueled my intent for life, and it persisted into physicality eventually in the final forms of sickness, slavery, debauchery, wantingness and wanting for, all not-so-far-flung examples as the seeming opposites of the peace and prosperity I chased. However, something others would see as a weakness or as the basis for giving up on life, I found the way to God is not through seeking and eventually obtaining worldly pleasures, but in surrendering over the pursuit of worldly pleasures for the uncertain future of chasing after God. This and this alone is the only way to reach the highest goal – the end goal of realizing that God, the creator and sustainer of the universe upon universes, is not bought and paid for with accolades, but experienced subjectively and imminently through the gifts of recognized forgiveness, practiced humility, and solely within a surrendered life to a single master, and a master not characterized by anything the world has to offer.

If you seek to know the truth about God, the truth about why you're here, the truth about why this whole thing called life is where you find yourself, you'll never get there chasing after anything the world calls valuable. The funny thing is, after surrendering over everything that life calls important, after letting go of every want, desire, craving, hope and ambition, money, and all manner of worldly goods, not only did I come face to face with truth, but I've never been more prosperous in the way the world would see as valuable. As I write these words now, I have more financial blessings, more personal success, and more potential being realized than any other time in life.

The secret of happiness that almost no one else on the planet knows is this: if you desire a thing, your reward is the pursuit of a thing, not getting that thing, and the more you seek after worldly things, the less happiness you'll experience subjectively.

Acceptance is a quintessential, spiritual building block perfectly needed for any personal foundation free from fear as a dominant, experiential subjective reality. Acceptance does not mean that one simply lays down their life for injustice or rolls over for hate. However, once one accepts that even injustice and hate hold no power over the slightest bit of love, acceptance is able to take on a holy and transcendental quality which no "march for peace" or "rally for human suffrage" could ever hope to accomplish for the individual's growth and future knowingness.

At a certain level of consciousness, acceptance is second nature, and quite honestly is as common as breathing, because once one has transcended being a slave to the ego and reached the beginning stages of pre-enlightenment, acceptance is life constantly unfolding before the witness of the eternal experience of now, because one is aware that everything is happening without one's personal input to start with, and everything is karmically perfect the way it is without needing to be changed for more perfection to be apparent. Whether you find yourself looking to shed some of the fear you're carrying around or your intent is fixed on reaching enlightenment, acceptance is paramount for success, for without it, experiencing the reality of God as imminent remains impossible for the person.

Accept that you have no control over anything except your choice matrix in this current moment, accept that tomorrow is uncertain and yesterday is gone, accept that changing someone else is not your job and is not within your power, accept that you are an experiential, witnessable, and observable aspect of God while in human form, accept that life is a vastly different experience for every other person walking on this earth than it is for you, and lastly you'll need to accept that your thoughts mean nothing, and you never were nor ever will be better than anyone else, but also not less than, with neither being equal in a worldly sense as an option. If you do this, you're on your way to the inner eye suddenly opening wide. If you can start accepting these truths on a moment-to-moment basis, even as the ego works to persuade you otherwise, then and only then will fear start losing its power over you for good. And yes, at this point, once the inner eye opens fully, beyond the start of the opening of the third eye of the Atmic Body, lust and greed no longer exist as anything controllable in one's experiential, subjective reality. To summarize: acceptance is key for spiritual growth.

Everything spoils and everything blooms, everything starts and ends, begins and finishes, inhales and exhales, but what most people never see is that this cycle happens simultaneously all the time, everywhere and nowhere all at once. All around us is Life, and all of Life is perfect in its expression. Everything that "we" are is made up of Life, as well as everything we think we're not and everything we're sure we'd never be. It's all Life. Each and every decision a person makes expresses Life, and Life is even present in-between the decisions as well as before the decision ever came to be. Every connection made strengthens Life's bonds between expressions of Life. Every kiss received sweetens Life's experience. Every dollar made expresses the value of Life currently in the experienceable physical world. Every dollar spent demonstrates the context of Life's many choices. At a certain point, examples are no longer necessary to recognize that Life, is spelled with a capital L, and not its lowercase version. Eventually, the spiritual seeker stumbles upon the understanding that everything is no(thing) in particular, but the entirety of everything simultaneously. As long as a person remains sure of the fact that something outside of himself is where happiness is found, the person will continue to miss the point of Life being all there is worth finding, and they will continue to lust after the next shiny object, only to miss out on truly experiencing the divine pleasure of Life found from looking within.

Life is always Life, it does not pass away, and only because of a person's narrow view of what's taking place around them, few ever see what's as obvious as breath coming from breathing – Life only perceptually changes form. There is nothing outside of Life, for how can someone see that which isn't possible for them to see? Take heed to these words to follow - nothing exists outside of Life, just as no(thing) exists worth more than Life. All of Life is on display at all times, and when the person keeps looking for happiness from a source other than that which gave life to them in the first place, they'll continue walking along unaware that Life is with them every step of the way, both blooming and spoiling, starting and ending, beginning and finishing, all the while inhaling and exhaling patient persistence. Only Life brings forth more life, and without Life there would be no choice at all.

INSTRUCTIONS FOR STEP EIGHT:

The vast majority of the work for this step was already done by completing the fourth and fifth steps. For this step, in relation to the fourth and fifth, we look back over the names of the people, places, things and institutions we have harmed or done damage to overtime by allowing the darkest aspects of our egos to take over our decision making. From the lists you already have, make a new list solely of the people who you feel you harmed during your life on this earth, then the places where you held resentments towards, the things you had anger towards, and the institutions you held grudges towards or wronged in any way. Once you have this list, do nothing for a few minutes but look over it. After taking a few minutes to look over it, write at the top of the page a new prayer similar to the fourth step one but with some additional wording: Lord, please help me see what needs to be seen so that what needs to be surrendered can be surrendered, and where I need to make things right you can make things right.

Now, look over the list again with this new context added to the mix. Then scan down the page of your list and make a check mark on the ones who you feel don't need an apology of any sorts or need to be made whole in any way. The names that are left require another few minutes of observation, as well as an internal prayer applied to them: please allow me to be *willing* to make an amends to these people, places, things and institutions, even if I don't feel like I'm able to now. The list you have left is what we'll take into the next step.

STEP EIGHT

-

Made a list of all the people, places and things I harmed along
the way and am willing to make an amends to them all.

STEP EIGHT PRAYER

-

Thank you for showing me what needs to be cleaned up from
my past. Please help me have the courage to be willing to make
right what needs to be made right. Thank you for the gift of
honesty and for the gift of courage. I love you.

Chapter 9

EXPERIENCING REASON
Walking the talk...

Step nine, making direct amends where possible, only doing so without causing injury to myself or others, is the second most feared step in the entire program, but also happens to be like the fourth step, in which both have the innate power to transform your life for the better. The reason both of these steps appear on their face to be scary, is because the ego works to bring about fear surrounding something that has the opportunity to create added freedom.

The ego is a smart and cunning conspirator to life until it's just a part of life and no longer what you allow to control decision making. Meaning, whenever something in your life has the likelihood of bringing you peace, clarity, evolved consciousness, or the chance at further happiness, the mind starts bringing up all the reasons you should be scared of something and should choose to make another choice about something. This is not done to persecute you, but done to show you the way towards freedom. The ego plays its hand every time it brings up a degree of fear in your awareness, or anytime your thoughts stray towards ways to hide or not tell the truth. There is no mountain peak without a valley, and there are no mile-high views without first having to climb somewhere to reach them. The ego is the valley, the 12-steps are the climb, you are the climber, and the views are the awareness of higher truths.

It is no coincidence that when you have something coming up in your life that will be seen as a blessing in hindsight, the mind starts bringing up all the possibilities about how it could fail, turn out bad, crumble between your fingers, or just not happen at all. The ego and the lower aspects of it can often feel prosecutorial, but in reality, they present a pathway towards truth through surrender. There has never been a time in my life where significant good happened without first having some degree of fear surrounding the moments leading up to it, and the same is said for this particular step in the program.

When I was getting ready to work through step nine in my own experience with these steps, I heard people all around me say how freeing the experience would be, how cathartic the experience would be, and how much healing would come from the completion of the step. But until I finished the step myself, I didn't have the knowingness that those voices around me were correct. Internally, what continued to arise before every person I had to make an amends with, a diffuse, internal awareness of fear surrounding what was about to happen would present itself. In every instance of making amends, despite the words that were part of the overall amends with a particular person, the end result was the same: gratitude.

This step and this chapter dealing with reason are part of the same thing: surrender leading to forgiveness, and forgiveness leading into gratitude. What you may or may not have noticed throughout the last five chapters of section two, and even with this step, we're putting forgiveness into action. In the first three steps of section one, we put surrender into action, and now we're headed towards putting forgiveness into further action once we take the last step forward into fully embodying forgiveness through step nine.

These steps were not originally designed, many years ago, to be broken up into three parts labeled Surrender, Forgiveness and Gratitude. This is only my observation of them in hindsight. However, the magic of the steps in being created is they embody these three characteristics baked into them. Separately, after completing the steps in totality, the realization came to me that my journey to the realization of the Self as God, could best be characterized as a three-step journey repeating itself over and over again which led to truth, with those steps being surrender, forgiveness and gratitude. These steps are where the power of change resides because these steps acquaint you with each component of witnessing God, and then they put those components of truth into practice, regardless of anyone recognizing the process unfolding. The magic is in the fact that these steps allow someone to put godly characteristics into practice through this format, and then habitually practice them moving forward in your daily life as spiritually based patterns of behavior. This step is the final culmination of learning what forgiveness looks like, understanding the significance of it, and then actively not only choosing forgiveness, but first accepting it and then practicing it.

Dr. Hawkins describes the characteristics of the level of reason as holding a view of God as wise, while seeing your life as meaningful. The main way someone at this level emotes within the world is as actively understanding how life works and how the laws of nature show merit and value. What also starts taking place at the beginning stages of reason is that deep down inside your being you start to witness that life is more than the concrete, more than the Newtonian definable world, more than what's seen. There begins to be the ability to see your decisions and fears are not rooted many times in validity or even investigative proofs. When you start this step there is a definite reason you're doing so, even if it just feels like you're doing so because the steps naturally lead to this point. But as you work through this step and finish it, you have an innate knowingness that something more important happened internally as a result of this step, and the reason for completing it wasn't just to check another box off the list.

The level of reason and the degrees to follow until arriving at love subjectively, take you through the Newtonian paradigm of existence, and bring the spiritual traveler squarely against having to take another leap of faith to progress into love and beyond, with that faith point being surrendering over the belief that causality is the highest form of likelihood and probability in the Universe. Meaning, is science the highest function of life, or is science an aspect of life which has a larger context from which it arises? Also meaning, is the brain and corresponding thoughts, feelings and emotions, what I am, or am I something that witnesses and observes these things take place? Within the level of reason comes scientific breakthroughs and discoveries beneficial to the human body and the physical world, but what also gets created are more and more ways to harm another individual, as well as more and more seemingly valid reasons to hold grudges against other people. The problem with the intellect is that it has a limit to its cognition, with the limit being that which expresses itself outside of the normal operations of the brain's functioning. The level of reason is also known as the level of the intellect, with this being the final calibrated level of consciousness to be transcended before one has the ability to know they're more than the mind, but less than all there is.

Just like the shared fear many have for this step, a similar question arises in choosing to complete it: do I know what will take place once I make an amends, or do I have to choose faith that what will come from the amends process is greater than what I think I already know?

A reasonable person would admit there is more to life than what they know, and logic would state that there's almost an infinite amount of learning possible over the course of a lifetime. So, how could you possibly know what will happen after you make an amends if you've never made one? And in this paragraph, you have now seen the ability to logically choose faith.

The truth is, we aren't what we think we are. We're actually closer to that which allows for thought to even be possible. In ultimate reality, we're not what we believe ourselves to be or how science defines us, but that which is the context for definition to even arise out of. Reason is a high level of consciousness, and it is possibly also the hardest level of consciousness to transcend, because to do so you have to be willing to surrender your attachment to thinking your way to God and to the beliefs that God is found through religion. God is not experienced in the mind or in a book, only described and acknowledged there through words. Love is not found in the mind, in the brain, in your emotions, feeling and thoughts, but only experienced as outside of all that and separate from any functioning of the mind at all. If you desire to truly know God as opposed to just think that God exists, one has to be willing to lay down what they think is their life to God and choose faith in the unknown currently.

Luckily, the last three steps of this program create a context of understanding gratitude as more than a word and concept, and because of such will be something you'll get to experience the effects of as opposed to just read about. In the levels that comprise reason, the individual inhabiting this space will be brought face-to-face with the reality that God is beyond explanation, that infinity is beyond the mind's ability to witness, and that the love you feel as a result of working these steps does not have a quantifiable degree of definition within the world of science that does it justice, or that compares in the slightest to an actual experience with the creator beyond what reason says is possible. Logic is born out of reason, but even the highest degrees of logic fall woefully short of actually subjectively experiencing the reality of divinity when it presents itself. At twenty, when divinity first presented itself to me in ways unknown before then, there was nothing logical or reasonable about what was taking place. God was just there in a way that the moment before God was not. When you find Truth, you will realize that lesser truths pale in comparison.

Again, the mind and the ego are the same thing, and the ego/mind believes itself to be God. The only way to see that the ego/mind is not God is to fully surrender it over to a power greater than yourself with the faith that what I say here is true about the outcome: God is not found in the mind, but quite naturally outside of it, and because of this fact, it's safe to walk straight ahead no matter what, constantly surrendering over your attachment to this world and all its trappings, because the end result of transcending the ego is not death but Life.

TRUTHS:

(The Gospel of Thomas) *Be wise like the fisherman who caught many fish. He kept the biggest fish, and returned the rest to the sea.*

147

(**The Dhammapada**) *Studying many scriptures is pointless if one does not practice the wisdom contained within them.*

(**The Bhagavad Gita**) *I abide in hearts out of compassion, replacing ignorance and darkness with a shining lamp.*

(**Chuang Tzu**) *Perfect wisdom comes spontaneously to those who seek it.*

CONTEMPLATING ON TRUTH:

Wisdom comes as a thief in the night, never announcing its arrival, but when it becomes apparent there's an outdated belief that lost its importance due to the arrival of a new contextual understanding, the house of the patron is left forever changed and altered in some unseen but subjectively felt way. However, unlike a thief, wisdom doesn't remove anything, instead, it leaves giving more than it took. I never spent much time fishing growing up, although it was available as a regular activity, but the idea of leaving all the little fish swimming and only keeping the mountable fish was not lost on me. I grew up around fishermen and those who claimed to be such, for in the south and growing up on a river, tall tales of river monsters vary far and wide. In the world of fishing there are a couple different types of cast-men: those who keep everything without being worried by the size of the catch, and those who keep everything they believe is worth bragging about. The first group keeps everything because they're hungry or bored, malicious, or without a mentor who taught them the sport of fishing. However, the person who keeps the trophy fish does so for the purpose of pride and a sense of accomplishment, and rarely out of hunger or boredom do these men and women cast their lines amongst the still waters. What I never witnessed was a fisherman who kept only the single finest fish they ever caught, for how could they, it would take a lifetime to know the results. The funny thing is, the only difference between the second type of fisherman and the type of fisherman I never met, is wisdom. Isn't knowing for ourselves that we caught many big fish in our lifetime the reward in and of itself? And wouldn't one man's "biggest fish" be a different size from another man's "biggest fish?" When one embraces reason, they choose logic and rationale, as well as discernment and wisdom, and like the thief who comes at night, pride remains lost, but replaced with a higher truth. If a fisherman were only to recognize the fish they know could not be matched from a lifetime of pursuit, wouldn't it be reasonable that this man or woman would have mastered the art of fishing, or at the very least, realized along the way that fishing is but another way to find a tale worth telling for all to hear?

Is it not reasonable to assume that if someone ceases from daily movement and interaction, they have stopped pursuing actionable steps in their life towards betterment and improvement? Is it not also possible that within inaction there also remains the possibility of inner action happening continuously? This is the quandary of the masses when looking at spirituality, for is it better to be doing something the world can see or to be doing something within your being that only God is aware of? Has not Christian scripture noted that prayer and righteous actions should be done away from the view of prying eyes, and doesn't Hindu scriptures say that either path is in fact actionable?

So, what is a spiritual traveler to do with the notion that only putting to practice what is found within scripture is the higher road to pursue towards the experience of a union with the Self, or with divinity, or with God? The truth is, one cannot effectively and with knowingness have the awareness that both options produce the same result. Unless they've chosen a path and followed it to its conclusion. However, before one can know the truth of peace found within the seeming inaction of the enlightened being, they first have to put into practice what is found within holy scriptures and stop believing that reading what someone else says is all that's needed for finding inner peace. Right words, right action, right thoughts, and right intentions are not found solely in words, but one won't know that until they put certain words into practice every day. Just because someone can talk about God in a way you find intellectually stimulating, that person's words only point someone towards putting them into practice. If you find that a spiritual teacher is without practice and comes not from personal experience, it might be time to leave their flock and find another, for their words have neither action nor inaction in the realities of higher truths. Without doing what another person has done, one cannot speak from a place of knowingness about its efficacy. Without walking the footsteps of another who has gone before you, one cannot reach a level of consciousness where more is being accomplished through what the world sees as inaction, compared to the work of a million people actively moving through the world to gain praise for their actions. One must first put into practice that which an enlightened teacher shows them as actionable steps before having the opportunity to know that action and inaction are actually one in the same thing.

One of the greatest missteps to life that modern man has created for himself is in wrongly interpreting what Jesus meant by "experiencing heaven on Earth." As an entity who regularly experiences life as heavenly, meaning, from one perfect moment to the next perfect moment, I can officially say that from my experience, Jesus has been misunderstood to such a degree that his words of enlightenment with regards to living in a heavenly state have served to separate Love from the lover, and the practitioner from the practice of Love. As one moves up the evolutionary scale towards being one with that which created him, it becomes clear that more and more Love present is what produces heavenly outlooks and experienceable moments of heavenly perfection while on earth.

Krishna is stating something similar above by referencing compassion as the abode for his presence. Krishna was Love, as Jesus was Love, with both arising from the same source and both representing a perfected union with God. We all arise from the same source as well, but when we choose ignorance and darkness as opposed to acceptance and reason, we're separating ourselves from Love, and thereby choosing to live in a world where heaven is not a possible destination nor a state of regular experience. As long as fear remains a person's regular mode of operation and primary choice paradigm, Jesus will always be the person whom you don't understand and can't relate to, until ignorance and darkness are no longer chosen regularly. No man or woman can know that Jesus and Krishna were not here to be idolized and proselytized for but were here as examples of a path forward where all one has to do is follow their lead and do as they did. Heaven as a reality doesn't come easily, and it's not found behind judgment or holding resentments, but through regular surrender, constant forgiveness, and a willingness to register all gratitude as worthy of a paused moment of reflection. Only then, will Jesus and Krishna start to become fellow travelers on your journey towards your own union with God. And only then can you show the world through actions and not your words that both Jesus and Krishna experienced the same reality of God.

Once one reaches a level of love or above as their current state of reality, what was said above becomes more obvious. However, until one realizes that Krishna and Jesus were here to show the possibility of being, taking on the human form, heaven and compassion will remain over there and otherworldly. The fastest path towards Truth is surrender, forgiveness and gratitude, in that order and practiced relentlessly until they become part of every waking hour.

If one seeks understanding as the sole basis to create wisdom, they'll soon be left with less than knowledge. Reason dictates that one thing is not something else, hence, understanding is not knowledge, however, when understanding is put to the test and lived out, knowingness in equal parts becomes spontaneous. Perfect spiritual wisdom is not a fixed accumulation of points within a cause-and-effect paradigm, but it is a conglomerate of perfected clarities separate and apart from the Newtonian paradigm of scientific investigation, as well as immersed in it until that paradigm no longer has the capacity to contain it. Wisdom and the scientific method are independent of one another. They're different paradigms, with wisdom arising out of a context of subjective knowingness and set apart from time tested methods of accumulated data leading towards only comprehending a phenomenon; while the Newtonian paradigm seemingly continues to move along its calculated path to the unenlightened and towards an A leading to B causality. It might arrive at a point of understanding, but the only knowledge gained is strictly capable of only producing more science, not more subjective knowingness. The world of wisdom is not governed by "this thing causing that thing," and because of this fact, there will never be a scientific method for contextually creating wisdom, only a method for understanding an intellectual pursuit for the sake of a brain that also gave us Karl Marx and Joseph Stalin as leaders of countries and movements. If you seek wisdom above all else, it will be provided to you in spontaneous moments of perfect clarity, never found within causality, but always produced apart from the content most believe to be the real. Wisdom is not only for the aged of society but is open to all individuals brave enough to not settle for the run of the mill understanding of the agreed upon molecular make-up of a thing. The nature of God is not experienceable within science or religion, nor any other mechanism of the mind. Wisdom trumps knowledge every day in its power and usefulness, as knowledge trumps understanding, and yet wisdom would not be had without first having the awareness that knowledge of life's choices is mandatory for wisdom's sake. When wisdom arrives, it is not carried along by itself, for it springs up singular out of the lived experiences of subjective realities. Anything that arrives suddenly cannot be traced back to causality, it must arise out of a greater context. For life to arise it must come from Life, not from un-life.

INSTRUCTIONS ON STEP NINE:

With our list in hand, we make a plan to address the wrongs we committed towards the people, places and things that became apparent needing to be made right from the previous step. We do not go into our amends process to say "I'm sorry" for what was done, but to make the situation right moving forward. We accomplish this task by admitting the exact nature of our wrongs, which sounds like an apology, except we're not asking for forgiveness, only providing the information about how we believed we wronged the other entity. We do not make amends where it would hurt us or another person further from the offense committed. Meaning, if we cheated on another person and we feel that broke their heart, if they find themselves in a new relationship or marriage, we don't selfishly make a direct amends just to make ourselves feel better. If we stole from someone, we go into the amends as a way to be willing to pay back that which we stole, no matter how long it takes. We make an amends for the purpose of cleaning up our side of the street, all the while knowing God has already forgiven us for the wrongs we committed. God has also made our standing straight again, so the amends process is not about groveling and repentance. It's about admitting the nature of our wrongs in a manner where we address any elephants in the room. The process for an amends is straightforward: Call, text, email, or write the person you harmed and inform them you have been working through a 12-step program which has you now making an amends for past behaviors and decisions made. Then you ask them if they would be willing to sit down with you or talk over the phone and give you a chance to explain. If they say yes, make sure you have dates and times available for the occasion, but if those times don't work for the person, be willing to work around their schedule.

Many times, the other person won't reply or doesn't want to talk about anything, which is fine. Leave the person at their wishes and come back to it a while later. Once you find yourself in front of the person or talking to them over the phone, lay out the script for the talk: The person in the program speaks first and talks through all the issues they created and why (without the other person interrupting; they'll have plenty of time to talk); next, the person not in the program gets to talk all they want about what was just shared and whatever else they have on their mind about things (you don't talk or make excuses during this time unless asked to talk); next, you ask them what you can do to make it right (we do anything we can within reason, never becoming the property of another or putting ourselves in further stressed situations that could cause damage to us physically or mentally); lastly, thank them for their time and for the opportunity to make things right. We make amends in another person's home only if safe to do so, as in the case of family or old friends of the same sex. We make plans to meet in an occupied space where social interaction is normal. If the other person doesn't want to see you, or you feel as if talking to another person would bring about too much stress and burden for each party, a living amends is applicable. A living amends works like this: say, you cheated on someone and broke their trust – never cheat on another person again; say, you stole from someone – never steal again; say, you lied to another person about something important – work to be truthful in all dealings moving forward; say, you had a span of years where you used people only for sex to make yourself feel better – be honest with all sexual partners moving forward about your intentions and why you're choosing to sleep with them. This step is about making things right and cleaning up your side of the street with another person, place, thing or institution. If you have cheated the tax system for years, the proper amends is having your taxes done properly and paying the penalties associated with past choices. Do not make an amends to someone who you feel is dangerous or who has put you in compromising situations or could put you in compromising situations. The amends process is for cleaning up messes, and it is a safe environment for letting go of past baggage as well as working on not creating new baggage. People will be mad at you, upset with your past behavior, stunned that you reached out, and also delighted to be speaking again. Overall, once starting this step you will feel lighter and freer than you thought possible before this step began, and before it's over you'll start to embrace and understand more deeply what gratitude truly is.

If you find yourself making an amends and it turns south on you where your safety is at jeopardy, feel comfortable thanking the person for their time and leaving the interaction totally. In all my years of knowing people who do their amends, no one has come back with a horror story where they didn't feel safe, although at times the other party remains angry and bitter after the talk, the amends isn't about them finding relief from your actions, it's about you admitting the nature of your actions and how you see that they affected the person you're talking to.

STEP NINE

-

I made direct amends to who I could and where possible, only doing so free of injury to them, myself, and others in our life.

STEP NINE PRAYER

-

I have fear around this step and I have apprehensions about the relief possible from telling another how I wronged them. I surrender over this fear and these apprehensions. Thank you for the chance to clean up my side of the street.

SECTION THREE

-

Chapters 10 - 12

-

Gratitude

Chapter 10

EXPERIENCING LOVE
It's time to transcend understanding…

There are several goals for this book with regards to its creation:

1) provide insight and opportunity for someone to have the experience of God as imminent;

2) provide a context for the experience of God as Self;

3) provide a definable way to transcend the ego and arrive at a level of love or above in this lifetime.

Once someone becomes love, the rest is only a matter of time – meaning, the work of this book is done, and the rest is up to your intent and your karma for this lifetime. By reaching a level of love as your subjective reality of life, you have arrived at a point where what comes next is between you and God, and the degree to which you have the fortitude to run the final legs of the surrender race and arrive at victorious peace.

The 12-steps in and of themselves, as written in this book, have enough power to deliver someone from hell to heaven. Meaning, the first goal for writing this book, if the reader does and completes the steps integrously, has enough innate value to carry someone into an experience of God as real. The supporting information and commentary written throughout this book, apart from the actual steps, have the added authority of high degrees of truth which further provide a context for the power of the 12-steps. Lastly, the context of commentary and the steps taken together, absorbed, even if not understood, have the ability to deliver the reader directly into a level of love or above in this lifetime as a result with a high degree of likelihood.

This book makes no claim about delivering enlightenment into your life as a byproduct of reading it, but what it does do is point you glaringly in the direction of God through truth, as well as layout the roadmap for how to arrive at a final destination. If you have a desire to connect with God in many of the ways that Jesus connected with God, enlightenment is your goal, surrender is your first step, forgiveness is for everyone, and gratitude for the journey is what will keep you moving towards the destination.

The calibrated level of love is rarified air and where someone can find themselves calibrating innately if they chase after God without ceasing, and it's also the first time a person has the opportunity to experience more sunshine on their daily experience than they do rain, or in another sense, more happiness present than pain experienced. Based on Hawkins's map of consciousness, when someone is love, quite naturally their view of God is as a loving creator. The way this person sees life and interacts with life is benign, meaning, a natural disposition of grace and kindliness towards most of life. Their central emotional connection with life is reverence for mankind, for life, and with a natural degree of forgiveness emanating forth as their disposition towards life. Quite possibly, the greatest gift of calibrating at the level of love, is the fact that revelations about God, the universe, mankind, and the Self, all start matriculating into awareness as more regular occurrences, creating prolonged mountaintop experiences and immediate realities of God as real and prominent in all things.

What happens from calibrating as love and moving on to even higher states, is through love you have the contextual understanding and firsthand experience with divinity needed to reach what's known as christhood, or through Hawkins's map of consciousness, a calibrated level of consciousness of unconditional love. Without love being present as a reality first, there are not enough regular occurrences with truth to provide the experiencer with the realizations that only continued surrender and forgiveness will take you to what's next. It is only through intensive and radical-based subjective honesty, can one reach the doorway of unconditional love through a surrendered life. To move on from love into higher dimensions, one first has to be willing to let go of all victimhood and be willing to forgive everyone for everything. You start that process by witnessing how God forgave you for what you thought at one point was unforgivable, and then use that understanding as the basis for projecting out the realized gift from firsthand experience to the world around you. It's at the level of unconditional love where Christ's words of "forgive them for they know not what they do" begin to provide actual context for daily living.

As I was going through this level of consciousness, the other thing that marks its reality is that suddenly, unexplainable phenomena start arising that present themselves as if out of nowhere, that are now with you for a moment but not for continued moments, which act like doorways into much higher dimensions of consciousness. At the level of love, you start to see higher truths in glimpses which are fleeting but instructional, and it's the truth of these glimpses that help propel you ever onward and upward towards the next set of heights worth climbing. In essence, once you have moments with God, you can't not want more time where God is present in ways you never thought imaginable. Love as your level of interacting with the world around you is the first time as a person where you have transcended a complete attachment to the ego. You have not, however, transcended it in totality.

This step is designed to deliver someone into regular and right standing with divinity, by making life a continual practice of surrender, forgiveness and gratitude. Once this current step of the 12-steps is completed and practiced daily, you can now speak about the reality of gratitude firsthand in your everyday experience of life. Once you have walked through the fear of talking to someone about how you wronged them, by admitting those wrongs openly and then walking away with your side of the street cleaned, you know gratitude is a byproduct of faith in action and not just an occasional emotional set.

In this step, we make surrender and forgiveness a daily exercise, which in turn will create a context for understanding how to use gratitude as a driving force moving forward. Also, because of where we are in the steps, one can start to see that through the surrender process and the choice to forgive yourself, God and the world around you, gratitude starts naturally arising as a state of awareness, like what thoughts, feelings and emotions once arose as.

Gratitude for being forgiven is what propels the person forgiven into a world where they are now able to forgive where needed and admit when they were wrong without the fear of judgment. This step is about constantly coming face to face with humility, and in admitting we are not perfected beings while in this body capable of never making a mistake again, but what we are is found in the knowingness that we come from that which created us. This knowingness separates all lower levels from the level of love, as well as the experiencer of life from the witness of life unfolding naturally around you.

If you desire to know God, set your intent on being love. Once becoming love, surrender over ever reaching unconditional love and enlightenment and ask God to accept a new intent of transcending even love to know God more fully. To reach unconditional love requires several things, but for the purpose of this book we'll look at the most important one:

forgiving everyone, all the time, for everything, no matter what.

This doesn't mean you have to take part in another's folly again and again, but it does mean you understand and acknowledge that all must be forgiven for the sake of the person doing the forgiving, mainly because "they know not what they do" to start with. I came to this realization when I fully knew that God had forgiven me for choices made when I knew not what I was doing. The only sin for mankind is ignorance, everything else is a byproduct of such, and it's through ignorance that fear-based decision making is chosen time and time again, with the byproduct of fear being destruction and devastation, judgment and anger, wrath and resentments, pain and suffering, desiring and craving, wanting and lusting, all to end with more pain and culminating in creating more fear. Fear leads to more fear, never to God. One does not find God through sackcloth and ashes, one starts to see God everywhere once they realize their creator does not require sackcloth and ashes for repentance. God does not judge you, you judge you. When you freely give forgiveness, without wanting anything in return, you quickly realize freedom and God are one in the same thing.

With this step, we have a new daily practice for putting forgiveness into action, humility into perspective, and gratitude into the awareness of who we are on a daily basis. Once you have found yourself on a regular basis forgiving the world around you, forgiving yourself, forgiving God, and forgiving another before they ask, you're in rarified air and amongst angels in human form.

At the level of love, beauty takes on a new form as well, and don't be surprised if sunsets bring tears to your eyes, or if the sight of two people in love stops you in your tracks, or if you find yourself unable to speak when certain music plays, for when you're love you recognize such everywhere in the world, and the recognition of love when you look out into the world is nothing short of miraculous every time it's witnessed.

TRUTHS:
(Chuang Tzu) *A wise man teaches others without using words.*

(The Apocryphon of James) *Seek wisdom earnestly through learning. Practice wisdom by being faithful, loving, and charitable.*

(The Dhammapada) *The body is a fragile thing. It must be protected against evil by the strong walls of wisdom.*

(The Upanishads) *Understanding immortality, those who are wise do not seek for truth among those things which are impermanent.*

CONTEMPLATING ON TRUTH:

For many years, I believed I was just and right in teaching others about life before I truly went out and lived it with any definable merit. I had a yearning to be the Tony Robbins type, complete with a program guaranteed to produce positive results for better living, and I dreamed of the time when crowds would gather around my feet to learn from my teaching and worship at the altar of Mason. I held this notion in mind as the pinnacle for my passions, and I used other speakers from around the globe as inspiration, motivation, and as possibilities for how my life could play out, and for what life would look like when I arrived finally at completion and happiness.

I now laugh at such naivety, mainly because I know

that one man's path is never the same as another person's, but secondarily, what would another person's course of life be in comparison to finding out what this one has in store for you as the traveler? What one man does can only serve as a compass for another, never the actual trip in totality. What I searched for, prayed for, longed for, pleaded for, and downright lost my mind over, was a way to express love through words as opposed to factual experience, and even before I started to fully experience it, I wanted to tell others how to know truth as well. I was hoping to fake it until I made it, and not have the world know this about me. I wanted the end result of popularity due to creative wording, as opposed to the reward being the entity who is sure about the true absolutes of life for themselves.

Now, I no longer have the need for comparisons or for goals, ambitions, desires or any other form of wantingness to be like someone else or emulate their life. Today, through the gift of enveloping love and effervescent peace, what's inside of me as well as inside of you, is the prize for the hours spent toiling away at arriving at the destination of freedom. Love rescued me from the never-ending cycle of rebirth, pain, sickness and old age. Love pulled me from the depths of hell and then delivered me into the experiential reality of continual perfection and Love witnessed, and no longer love witnessed as a phenomenon of two people joined in attachment, but of the natural order of life where God is present in ways many never get to see for themselves. Love, and only Love, is what the journey is for - to express it, experience it, feel it, touch it, think it, witness it, observe it, and then eventually be it. If you live a life dedicated to the pursuit of Love, you'll find your "it" when you're ready, and you'll find that it was never in the direction towards crowds gathered at your feet to begin with.

During the early years of my life, I pursued a spiritual understanding that went far beyond book learning and classically styled research. For most of my adolescent life, more years than not, I had an unyielding intent to reach the truth about life, religion, and the point of it all, which I pursued with a reckless abandon in doing everything I could to reach truth. However, more than wanting answers to the aforementioned points of interest, I needed to know what God was and is, did God exist, why was I here, and what is this place we call earth all about with regards to being human? Then, after finding a direct awareness of God at age twenty, I spent twelve years doing my best to forget I ever had these questions answered, but thankfully for me, the past can only stay hidden for so long. At twenty years old, I had my first glimpse of the reality of God in the form of experiencing the knowingness that God is, but I didn't have the life experience yet to fully comprehend the ramifications of this realization.

So, as I said, I spent years out on the lamb after that experience with innate divinity, doing my best to turn over every rock and squeeze every ounce out of life to find out what was the real truth, and not the truth someone else was selling. After finding myself squarely in hell, twelve years searching for language about God again out in the world, I woke up and decided I had gone long enough trying to hide from the questions which defined my childhood, sculpted my adolescence, matured my young adulthood, and now found my journey had delivered me squarely back to the question of what God is. To my amazement, God never forgot about me or my lines of questioning, and once I became ready to pay attention, God showed off and reminded me that love is the backdrop for all of everything there is that's observable and unobservable. Along the way, I asked for a definition of what we all are, and the answer to that came as well: "I, in greater or lesser degrees of intensity."

Which led to my next question, "What is "I," exactly?" The reply was, "God, known through Love, experienced, witnessed and observed through consciousness."

Upon further reflection, subsequent raises in consciousness levels, and an experienceable reality currently which justifies such bold writings as these, love continually shines through as all there is we can experience of God, because love is how we get to have awareness of God, in lesser or greater degrees of intensity. We know God through love and we know God because of love. God is not found in fear, or judgment, or resentments, or any other manifestation of the lower mind. God is known because of love, through acts of surrender, forgiveness and gratitude, eventually presenting the reality that God is all there is.

The physical body is nothing more than a vessel for experience to matriculate from. The physical body is fragile compared to that which created and sustains it. The physical body is limited compared to that which created it. The physical body is prone to disease and death, unlike that which created it. The physical body is what most people believe they are. The physical body is nothing more than a bag of meat, bones, along with a supercomputer, all working together to create the proper conditions allowable for experience to appear singular and separate from another.

We are not our bodies, but most believe they are. We are not our thoughts, but most believe they are. We are not our feelings and emotions, but most believe they are.

The physical body allows the witness of experience to have a subjective reality of localized consciousness. The body is subject to the mind until it is not any longer. The mind is a receptor point for consciousness and the ego alike. The body will create within itself what the mind holds as allowable and permissible. The body will move forward against evil only when the witnesser of experience has the intent to do so. The body is subject to karma and what the witness holds in mind to be true, and because of this, effects of fear are often misinterpreted as credible, and then act as aids to the manifestation of a weak mind-body experience. If the mind is allowed to remain in the gutter of negative and despondent thinking, of false witnessing, of chosen ego, the body will follow with disease, pain, injury, depression, and eventually motivated expiration.

The body is a fragile thing, and the way to protect it is seeking Truth in all its forms above believing in feelings in all their illusory forms. Truth makes the body strong and falsehood makes the body go weak. Truth gives the body energy and falsehood drains one's physicality. When a person decides to move towards truth in their pursuit of understanding and experience of life, the body naturally follows the mind's loving lead, and never the other way around. From ashes the body arises and to ashes it returns, but what we truly are never dies or extinguishes, it only transforms into whatever consciousness experiences and witnesses/observes next. Be not in love with your body but have love for the body. Be not attached to the body for such a thing only brings pain. When you truly know you are not the body, you have realized a great truth. When you know you're not the mind, freedom is close.

Understanding immortality is made clear when the person seeking to understand life and death lets go of his/her attachment to anything physical in nature, and then seeks to understand that the non-physical elements of inquiry present an attachment as well. Understanding immortality, without fully living a life where attachments and expectations of all things content driven are better left in a past life, is like learning how to swim on dry land, while continually asking yourself why it is the sand is not more waterlike. Is it possible to know about water from the vantage point of dry land? Yes, but not conducive to actually swimming in it. Is it possible to watch someone swimming and get an idea for how it's done? Yes, but in this case, you're not the one having to stay afloat. Is it even possible to practice your strokes while fixed to the shoreline and have an idea of what it feels like to swim? Yes, but the feelings are only best-guesses.

Contemplating immortality and experiencing immortality are entirely different paradigms of existence. The person who seeks to know the nature of God is on the path to experiencing God. However, being on the path is not knowing the scenery of the destination, but only the steps currently taken. When you decide to let go of attachments and expectations to your beliefs of God, the nature of man, and the reasons for existence, you won't have to try and understand Life anymore. You'll start fully experiencing it to the point where floating above water is effortless and witnessing Life and Observing Life take on degrees of buoyancy rather than lead-laden shoes.

To those who are wise among us reading this thought here, and for those who are reading this thought and desiring wisdom in their life, either beginning scenario can create the same end where one knows what it is to swim: understanding trumps guessing, experiencing trumps understanding, knowingness trumps experiencing, and witnessing/observing as byproducts of knowingness allows for immortality to become evident. Seek truth for its own sake and without attachment to what's found, and soon experience will present itself in a way where guessing about what comes after physical death is no more a part of your knowingness than trying to swim while still affixed to the soil, which only ever butted up to the water.

INSTRUCTIONS FOR STEP TEN:

This step can be performed in several different ways, with the first being at the end of each day, looking back over the day, for moments you judged another, lied, need to forgive another or be forgiven by another, were quick to anger with someone, gave your opinion unsolicited to another person, or otherwise didn't treat another as you would wish to be treated.

Once seeing these instances, agreeing to reach out to these people and admit where you were wrong, or working these instances through the 4th step matrix and presenting your findings to the person you wronged the next day.

Either way, this step is about admitting where we fell short of grace during the course of the day, and then taking immediate action where possible to ask for forgiveness and practice humility. In my daily practice of this step, in every moment, surrender is facilitated where applicable, and when possible, in the moment, seeking innately to remedy the situation.

STEP TEN

-

Endeavor to do both daily, take personal inventory and where I'm wrong, quickly admit it.

STEP TEN PRAYER

-

I surrender over my desires to be right, to be appreciated, wanted, desired, thought highly of, and all desires to be better than another or lord over another.

Chapter 11

WITNESSING JOY
Staying connected with truth...

Every morning upon waking, as awareness returns, I surrender the day over to God through inner words of prayer and supplication. Every night before the body falls asleep, on bended knees I pray and thank God for the day and once again surrender life over. Throughout the day, as anything from the collective which is ego-based arises into awareness it gets immediately processed as an "other," and then promptly all attachment to what arose is surrendered over as well. Almost every moment of everyday life is spent in constant contact with God in one of three ways: surrender, forgiveness, or gratitude. This may sound like a lot of work to many of you reading this, but the reality is, once becoming internally aware of being something outside of the experiencer edge of the ego, once knowing you're more akin to the witnesser and observer of life and less the thing that experiences the content of life, everything that arises throughout the day becomes more like watching it unfold on TV and having the awareness of the channel changing effortlessly without any control over it, except there's always the same thing watching it, "I." The fact of the matter is, no matter where you find yourself consciously and no matter one's level of consciousness, what the world sees as the person, is not in control of anything happening around them. You're simply watching life unfold with either a degree of attachment to it as "your" life, or actively surrendering over the attachment to it as Life, and then finding peace in this knowingness.

The eleventh step is about already having your side of the street clean and swept up daily, having surrendered over your will for life to that of a higher will for your life, and for receiving forgiveness as well as giving forgiveness in all capacities requiring it. When we arrive at this step, after first completing the previous ten, what we have is the decree to maintain our daily contact with God as we understand God, or in another parlance, continually surrendering over the lesser to the greater. Through prayer, meditation, contemplation, witnessing the awareness of life, sitting quietly and observing nature and/or the workings of life going on around you, or any other form of allowing oneself to acknowledge that there is indeed something greater in the world that you arose from and currently operate within. We strive daily to humble ourselves before the greater context of life, for the benefit of staying connected to love and its many blessings, as opposed to staying stuck to the belief we are a slave to fear and its propensity for destruction.

By this point in the steps, what you'll notice taking shape in your life, is your outlook has shifted a little bit or a lotta bit for the better, and now the needs of others are intrinsically important to you, at least to the degree that you recognize them as valid emotional sets and important aspects of being human. If these steps and the surrender process in general have brought you into a world where the corresponding level of consciousness known as unconditional love is seen through your eyes as a current lens for witnessing life, you've already noticed your daily routine has become one that comprises more service naturally to others and the world around you than at any point you can remember. Unconditional love, as a calibrated level of consciousness, is one of the greatest levels a person can find themselves resonating with. It is during this level that the person has regular occurrences with the awareness that God not only exists, but can be seen almost everywhere you look.

At this point, you still don't know what God is, but there is no doubt left that God is real, because all around you is the innate recognition of some degree of beauty, harmony and perfection breaking through with every glance of the eyes.

At this level of consciousness, you start finding it harder to relate to the world around you as a definer of what you are, with the world projected in the media and in the twenty-four-hour news cycle unfolding more like a play you watch but aren't a part of. You'll find yourself, at this level, unsure why the rest of the world acts the way it does, or why people treat others without kindness and respect as the first option of business. With each new day that passes, you'll fall further and further away from the trappings of the material world and all its content and become more and more filled with awe in relation to the presence of God becoming close and personal.

As one progresses through the elevated levels of unconditional love, sainthood arises as an aspect of reality, but not something you observe about yourself, but as a characteristic of what naturally has become your disposition and way of life which others see as just the way about you. At the higher levels of unconditional love, you have found heaven on earth noticeable as the inner subjective experience of life from time to time. At these higher levels, the experiencer aspect of perception starts blending naturally into the witnesser aspect more and more, and seamlessly you find that something within your being draws you to places where the love inside of you effortlessly pours out in order to provide witness to miracles arising from your presence.

At this level, you also realize it is not what the world sees as you which provides miracles, but the immense energy of love that comes through you which heals the sick and gives life to the needy. At this level of consciousness, sickness is healed for the person who prays for it and has the karma allowable when they're in your presence. For yourself, at this level of consciousness, there is no longer an attachment to the sickness you may have carried with you into this dimension of life, and therefore your suffering from something has abated.

People don't perform miracles, but what they are in reality allows for the Holy Spirit to use their body as a vessel of its will to deliver the energy needed to a particular person or location when required for a miracle to be performed. God uses people to help people, but the person at this stage of consciousness gets used time and time again to do the heavy lifting of unanswered prayers. Again, the person isn't a miracle worker, what they are is the miracle that promotes further miracles. If you are more love than ego, you have the ability to be more for the world of what they need at the roughest of times as opposed to what they need to feel more like the world around them. At this level, you are less the world around you and more the higher will for your life playing out before your very eyes. Also, at this level, you'll find the mind slowing down in its constant need for clamoring about incessantly, and what's left is a quieted version of the ego only barely existing and not thriving.

Very few reach this level of consciousness, but that doesn't mean it is unobtainable. What I have noticed since chasing after God full-time, is the person who chases after God while forgiving the world around them is the same person who arrives at unconditional love as their subjective reality and lens for witnessing the way the world works.

Depending on one's level of consciousness, what they are determines the lens for which they view life, so when someone reaches the level of unconditional love, how they see the world is not more right than another person, it's just a way of seeing and interacting with the world where there are fewer clouds and less pain points than another. Set your sights on being unconditional love and you'll reach it in this lifetime, however, as we have stated before, the spiritual life is not for the weak minded or the traveler who is afraid of walking many miles.

The closer one grows towards higher truths the more baggage must be left at the loading dock. As one sets their intent on reaching God through sainthood, they've made a decision to allow the ego to go into full scramble-for-survival mode. Meaning, one does not reach higher levels of unconditional love through half-measures and minimal surrender. In order to surrender over what needs to be surrendered over to reach unconditional love, all that needs to be surrendered over must have the opportunity to arise and subsequently be let go of. One way to look at this is through the image of a surfer getting ready to catch a wave: first, the board must be in good working condition and be properly ready for action; second, the person on the board has to know how to surf; third, to make it beyond the break point where catching a wave is possible, the surfer must traverse breaking waves in his path and maneuver around and through them in a variety of ways, while nevertheless continuing forward through all the obstacles; and lastly, the surfer must arrive at the point where the sets roll in, while waiting for the right set to make its appearance so that all of the work in getting out there pays off.

Just like the surfer reaching the point where catching the perfect wave is possible, the spiritual aspirant must have a compass that works, the intent to use the compass, the fortitude and spiritual will to traverse all the obstacles, and the ability to see that what arises on their path is not meant to stop them from reaching God, but is in fact what stands before them in order to reach God. There is no room for half-measures when choosing to witness the splendor of God, and if you're not willing to let go of wrongs and spites or resentments over even the smallest thing, and surrender over every attachment and aversion to life in the process, you'll never know God as a regularity, instead you'll be the person on the beach watching the other person catch the wave always wondering what it feels like to surf.

From love to unconditional love the entire world changes for the subjective witnesser. It's not as if anything physically changes out in the world around you. It's that how you see the physical world takes on an entirely different dimension of awareness. For the moment at hand, we'll take a look at how Dr. Hawkins describes the changes happening at this level of consciousness: at unconditional love, your view of God is no longer as separate and apart, but as one with you. At this level, the way you see life is as complete without any needs going unmet. The way you carry yourself in the world is as full of a serene energy capable of facing any challenge head-on without judgment or contempt. The process by which your life operates at this level is one of transfiguration, meaning, what you are innately is now something utterly greater than the vast majority of the world walking around you. What you are is not better than another, but what you are is so full of love for the world, God, and your fellow man, that how you walk around this earth has been transfigured from being Homo sapiens to being something slightly different, and as something much more capable of staying this way.

To be unconditional love walking around in the human form, you have now reached a place where your life is becoming fully realized that it's not your own, but somehow a part of something grander, larger, and more meaningful than ages past.

TRUTHS:

(The Bhagavad Gita) *At the end of many births, the wise person takes refuge in Me - realizing that all things are the Self. Rare and wonderful is the soul that achieves this state of consciousness.*

(The Tao Te Ching) *Wise is the person who has no preferences for one thing over another. He allows his heart to become empty of desires.*

(The Gospel of Matthew) *Who, then, is the faithful and wise servant, whom his master has set over his household to give them their food at the proper time? Blessed is that servant who remains faithful, for the master will set him over all his possessions.*

(The Dhammapada) *Those young in dharma may lose their vigilance, but those who are wise guard it carefully - for they treasure it above all things.*

CONTEMPLATING ON TRUTH:

A person will believe something to be valid only as long as their sight stays fixed on that thing as worthy of investment, or until a higher degree of truth is witnessed and imprinted which replaces the lower hanging fruits. Something magical happens to the witnesser once their eyes gaze off into the distance, past the confines of another's teaching, and what stares back at them is the Self, quietly imploring the seeker to let go of what is now old understanding being replaced by current wisdom.

Something happens to the witnesser once their ego is properly seen for what it is and then efficiently disposed of with regards to any attachments to it as ultimate reality. Something happens to the witnesser once there is no experience of chosen attachment and/or expectations left, and all that sits in the ever-evolving moment of now is the reality that the Self is all there is, beyond understanding and approaching, with only realizations turning immediately into knowingness. Something happens to the witnesser once they realize they never were and somehow always are, and yet always will be, despite currently having what appears to be a body with limits of interacting with life. Something happens to the witnesser once formal religion no longer plays a role in their spiritual development, and what comes forth from their beingness is not a need to follow the teaching of a book or a pastor, and instead they become the truth found in a book and the words spoken by the pastor. Something happens to the witnesser once Life is seen as all there is and there is nothing but the Self in all beings and all things, all the time without end, forever and ever amen. Something happens to the witnesser once witnessing has lost its illusory form and now presents itself as the opening doorway to observing the reality of God unfolding without end, always moving and shaping into another creation and creative being. Something happens when the witnesser relates to what is being witnessed. They begin living for the first time from the opening viewpoint of the Self, and not from the confines of what they once believed their self to be.

I have come forth in many births and I will live on once this mortal flesh loses its grip on this plane. I have found refuge in God as the only reality there is, realizing all things are the Self, and how wonderful it is to witness life from a vantage point clear of debris.

When one's attachment to wants and desires becomes part of the past, and when joy is naturally present in the moment-to-moment of the passing nowness of everything that is, one has become wise in their decisions. But only once all attachments to what was, are now replaced with the surrender of what is, can one witness the freedom that comes with having a heart empty of positionality. Wisdom is not found in worrying about when joy will present itself, for true wisdom is held vibrant in the time when attachments and aversions have left the moment of one's current experience, with the byproduct of such being the awareness of not only joy present, but the willingness to turn over even joy to the creator through surrender.

Joy is not something chosen through the murkiness of everyday life by simply saying to oneself, "Now, I will choose joy over sadness." Instead, joy is the byproduct of surrendering over the preferences of one's animal nature for the hidden treasures of context becoming clear, and clear to the point of awareness allowing joy to be naturally present as that which is left once preferences no longer remain. As long as there are attachments to, and expectations of wants and desires, the state of not hoping for one thing over another without judgment will not be possible as one's experiential reality, and because of such, the gift of subjectively realizing that joy is not just experienced periodically, but actually part of the ever-present nature of God that resides continually within and among all things, will not become known.

When joy is allowed to arise naturally, it can be witnessed as though it is a kind breeze flowing gently against one's cheek, momentarily there and gone again only to return when conditions are propitious, however, not held onto for the sake of the moment, but appreciated for its eternal nature which extends beyond the here and now. Joy is an evolved aspect of love, and love is the precursor to joy, and without the springboard nature of love, joy would not be available as a reality. With the embodiment of unconditional love as one's subjective reality, comes the inspiring awareness of joy as a more constant state, surpassed only when the witnesser of such chooses to surrender over even joy, for faith in the opportunity that allows for what's next to take shape. Joy is not just something that a person gets to feel occasionally, but a subjective reality constantly for the person who has no preferences for one thing over another, and whose heart has become empty of desire.

There was once a time when I was master of nothing but sadness. There was once a time when I was master over only rage, envy, greed, lust, grief, anger, resentment, guilt, regret, shame, and all other forms of lesser-than factors which are byproducts of a life lived as a slave to the ego. I was master of not only the lesser aspects of the human experience, but I was master over their promulgation, along with their manifestation from moment to moment and the effects of such lower levels of human existence. I was neither faithful to God nor a cause, nor willing to be a servant of either, nor did I reside in a household providing food and nourishment other than the home I built out of the bricks and mortar that the world would have me believe was a worthy and justified foundation – a home built on the banks of a changing river. For any transcendence of the lesser aspects of humanness to take place, I had to first surrender over the lesser of life currently experienced for the prospect that faith in the unknown greater might indeed allow such un-pleasantries to exist in my knowingness no longer.

One cannot understand the opportunity for change without having the faith required to be willing to take the steps necessary for change to happen. Without the willingness to be a servant of God as opposed to the servant of baseless desires, one will never know what joy is, let alone peace, harmony, happiness, wonderment, miracles, honesty, freedom, and a constant connection with the source of all such things. When one humbles themselves to the reality that no servant is greater than their master, then at that point one will realize that it is more than enough to be like their master, and when one becomes like their master, all possessions will not only be given to him, but all possessions will freely flow from him to another walking in his shadow. The blessed servant is actually the master of much, but because serving is the mechanism to acquire riches in heaven and not gold on this earth to be hoarded, that which is possessed is not held tightly, but freely shared through the act of stewardship granted to him in the first place. The person for whom much is given, has the opportunity to be the source of the blessings where much is given away. God knows the heart of man, and those who think they can hide from God, the fact they look only to acquire as opposed to serve, little of value will flow into their life. I was once a master of little sustenance, until service dictated that much is now to be given away freely for others to find nourishment in.

Early on in the life of the sage, there is not always present the type of character which would be indicative of a holy person on the road to enlightenment. However, once the life has been lived and the person has arrived at holiness and has the realities that arrive out of such a worthwhile pursuit, what is changed in that person is now someone is present who regards righteousness as something worth guarding through continual surrender, as well as the innate knowledge that purity and the joy that comes from righteousness are the treasures worth storing in heaven.

In the case of the entity writing this passage, my youth was spent in varying degrees of frivolity, with little wisdom present in the way of guarding the treasure that is a union with dharma. As time progressed, and youth became early adulthood, the decisions of the child remained close to the surface, and yet again wisdom eluded the experiencer. From adulthood arose hell as a reality experientially, but from a certain point while in hell, a great change happened and heaven as a subjective reality became witnessed and observed. Once heaven became the experience in the ever-present moment of now, joy was no longer buried from the observer, but instead it was part of the reality that had become miraculous for each new breathtaking moment. Where there was understanding as a youth, knowingness as a surrendered adult replaced it. Where there was searching as a young adult, wisdom as a surrendered adult replaced it. Where there was a lack of vigilance as a wayward soul, a guard at the gate took its place through the gift of letting go of all attachments and aversions.

There is nothing left on this earth that could entice the observer from leaving the oneness with all there is - not the

186

promise of gold or riches beyond imagining. The miracle that started it all was not a lack of vigilance stopping joy from becoming regular, but a lack of humility finally surrendered over which allowed the experiencer new realizations, that joy and peace are not byproducts of a person who believes their life is their own, but a person who surrenders over even their life to the creator and sustainer of all that is. We don't own anything, and at best we're quality stewards of things. If you don't have the ability to recognize the fact that you are not God, you will never have the realization that you in fact are God, expressing Itself through your beingness and localized lens of consciousness. The kingdom of God is within, and that truth is worth being vigilant about while guarding carefully the inner peace that comes forth from proper stewardship of such a precious gift.

INSTRUCTIONS FOR STEP ELEVEN:

This step is all about being in the world but not of it, and thusly, living your life like a prayer. This is a step to be completed every day for the rest of your life, because this step is about regularly choosing God and continually saying goodbye to your attachments of the world in the process.

Saying Goodbye to the world does not mean you leave it entirely. It means you're always letting go of your attachments to what arises within it on a daily basis.

You can complete this step systematically through prayer, meditation, contemplation, surrender, forgiveness, gratitude, or all of the above. You can complete this step through service to the world around you as a display of your willingness to serve God by serving man, or you can stay connected to God through deliberate acts of devotion like completing these steps or sharing your experience of God with another person when asked to do so.

For the author, surrender in the morning, surrender throughout the day, and more surrender at night, sets the context for a conscious contact with the creator, while asking only for God's will for this life to manifest as what's chosen in every moment. For you the reader, it may not look like this, but have no fear about it one way or another, for this step is about choosing Love in any way you can throughout your waking hours. By choosing Love on a daily basis, you're completing this step.

How do we choose Love as opposed to fear? We do so by letting go of all the attachments we have, the wants, desires, hopes, aspirations, cravings and demands for life, and instead help where help is needed, pray when prayer arises, serve when service is an option, forgive instead of holding a grudge, and actively being grateful by recognizing life as a gift and not a curse.

STEP ELEVEN

-

Through surrender, forgiveness and gratitude, I continue to improve my conscious contact with Truth, Love, and all other characteristics of my Creator, praying only for God's will to be what guides my life, and for the power to carry out that will once presented.

STEP ELEVEN PRAYER

-

I surrender over my life to thee of Lord, the steps I take, the thoughts that arise, the beats of my heart, the manifestations of the ego and the workings of the mind.

Chapter 12

WITNESSING PEACE
Being the message…

As we move into this final step and completion of the program, we'll be looking at the entirety of this step from two different angles:

1) Completing the 12th step means having worked the previous eleven in order, and now arriving at the point where you are willing to take another person through the process when the opportunity arises – it also means agreeing to incorporate the 10th and 11th steps into your life as regular modes of operation for the remainder of your life.

2) Arriving at the doorsteps of enlightenment, and what it takes to make the final run towards the realization of God as Self.

We'll look at the first angle before we move onto the second lens for incorporating this work into your life. Reaching the twelfth step is no easy task, but neither is it a hard one if you started this program praying or begging for a way to create more closeness to God. The difficult nature of doing the work found in this book isn't because anything is physically demanding, but because in order to complete the steps one must choose faith many times over through the process of surrender, forgiveness, and gratitude, and one must be willing to abandon the notion of belief that what's found in the mind is the highest form of experiencing Truth.

The gift of the twelfth step, is that the program comes to an end as far as working steps are concerned, but from another angle, the program is truly just beginning. The program ends and yet begins at number twelve, because by this point, you have all the information needed to transcend the ego and fear in all of its forms, but in order to complete this step you have to be willing to take another through all twelve of them. Becoming someone's sponsor is not to be taken lightly, and along with agreeing to do so requires some rules both parties must follow:

- You as the sponsor, agree to take the next person through the steps the same way you were taken through the steps, not deviating from the process and/or creating new ways for completing them.
- The sponsor never does this work for payment or gratuity.
- The sponsor is not what works miracles in the life of another. They're simply walking the next person through the steps which delivers love to another more abundantly, and it's the love in abundance which creates changes for the practitioner.
- The sponsor is not a bank for the person they're taking through the steps, and is not to loan money to the stepper or provide housing or other financial means.
- The sponsor is not responsible for the next person finishing the steps, only being available and willing to walk them through the steps as time permits.
- All conversations between the sponsor and the person working the steps are kept between the two parties, unless permission is given to talk about experiences and conversations held.
- No sponsor proselytizes this work as a means to recruit next steppers, but he/she must be

willing to talk about their experience with the steps when asked by interested parties.

- There is never to be sex between the sponsor and the person working through the steps, for this relationship is meant to be platonic and not one of dominance.
- The sponsor only guides the next person through the steps, and never does the work for the person, always only sharing their personal experience throughout the process as a means for guidance.
- The sponsor works around the schedule of the person taking the steps, never demanding the work be finished by the stepper in a particular timeframe.
- The sponsor doesn't dictate the time it takes for someone to finish the steps, but can leave the relationship if their time is being abused by the person taking the steps.
- The sponsor is not demanding or for the purpose of placing any rules on the stepper, with his/her role only being a witness to their experience with the steps along the way, and as a guide for completion of the steps.

As far as further rules go, if more need to be added they will be with later publications and editions of this book, but for now, think of these rules as guidelines for a successful 12th step sponsor relationship.

The way someone becomes a sponsor is quite natural and easy but may not always look the same as another person's experience. Before this book is published, those choosing to work these steps will have a forum and community to engage with who can serve as sponsors, but as time progresses and more and more people finish these steps and share a new life with the world around them as a byproduct of their efficacy, there will be more people wanting to do the steps than people able and willing to sponsor them.

As in AA, this program is one of attraction and not promotion. As a community, we'll look at ways to work around the supply of sponsors and the demands of steppers. However, the easiest way to find someone to sponsor is by letting God know you're ready to finish the program and be a sponsor, and when the opportunity arises, let people know you're available to walk them through the program, while not shying away from doing so when presented an opportunity.

There will be much more information about the sponsor and stepper relationship via online resources and in-person meetings, but for now, I'll say one last thing about the gift and blessing of being a sponsor before moving onto lens two of this chapter: the blessing of a sponsor is mutually valuable to the sponsor and the person working through the steps, because only the sponsor, based on their unique vantage point, gets the gift of seeing another arise at truth and find clarity in the process. The sponsor and the stepper are mutually blessed in this process, and the time needed to sponsor someone pales in comparison to the value added in their life by doing so.

Enlightenment is talked about in many ways and from many angles, with most parties in today's world, not speaking from the subjective reality as experienced or witnessed truth, but from a place of reading about a change in perception from another's viewpoint. This reality creates mystification around the subject and not factual interaction with truth. The term enlightenment in its truest sense just means a highly elevated angle of perception, marked with a uniquely similar way for how the world is witnessed and interacted with, observed and experienced by all throughout time who have reached such a level of conscious awareness. In essence, enlightenment is a condition of perception more than a physical alteration of attributes or a vernacular of magical belief-based phenomenon.

No person becomes enlightened, because once the condition sets in, the belief of being an individual person evaporates and what's left is life without individual description as well as any attachment to the beliefs of duality or cause and effect. There are various levels of enlightenment just like there are various levels of schooling, with each one not better than another, but which build on one another through acknowledgment and evolved knowingness. When enlightenment sets in as one's new paradigm of awareness, the moment and corresponding moments to follow are undeniable and without total description both physically and spiritually, other than to say it is without question, was not present the moment before it presented itself.

If the entirety of the world and perception has not shifted in a way that leaves the experiencer changed forever to such a degree where knowingness has replaced thinkingness, and "I-ness" is not present as all there is, enlightenment has not taken place. You won't have to wonder if you're enlightened, because the moment it arises is without comparison to date physically as well as through the lens of awareness, and without confusion or worry involved. Pure ecstasy, unbridled connection, unbound peace, and the inability to be anything other than what's taking place, all converge and coalesce at the moment one finds their steps walking through the doorway of enlightenment, leaving behind any definition of self, replaced forever with the all-present knowingness that all is One, and life is more than imagined as possible only moments before.

Jesus the Christ was fully enlightened, as was The Buddha and Lord Krishna, as has been the case for others throughout millennia in varying degrees of intensity. The purpose of and innate experience with full enlightenment is not different in description for Jesus, the Buddha, Krishna, or others who have found their life forever changed by the innate knowingness at the highest degrees that God is in fact the Self, as well as everything else simultaneously, however, that does not mean that each person who realizes they are in fact that which created it, are here for the same purpose and outcome.

I mention the three people above to show the similarity for having an innate knowingness about God being all of life, but also to highlight their different reasons for taking on human form in the first place. Jesus incarnated for the purpose of providing salvation to mankind and to be an example of Love in human and sacrificed form. Krishna was Love in human form as well, but not to preach about heaven and salvation, but to teach about love and the pathway to God through the choices of action or inaction. The Buddha, unlike Jesus and Krishna, was not born enlightened, but realized enlightenment through his own determination for truth at all costs, and then taught his experience of reaching the truth of existence for the purpose of not having to reincarnate into physicality again.

All three physical manifestations of God were here to be examples and teachers, but all three had different ways of doing this and different languages and life experiences used to demonstrate their messages. All three individuals experienced the reality of divinity the same way, and because of their presence on this earth, as well as the presence of other enlightened beings throughout the ages, you too have the same opportunity to know that God is, as opposed to thinking God is probably real.

If you have a desire to change the world for the better, your only course of deliberate action should be to chase after Truth and pursue enlightenment, for every person that truly knows God and leaves just thinking about divinity behind, is another person who is in the world but not of it, and when you're in the world but not of it, you change the world for the better by simply existing. You raise the levels of the sea for all of mankind so every boat floats easier in the water without even realizing it. What you are emanates out from the presence of what you are in varying degrees of intensity as well, so when fear and anger comprise your reality, you spread fear and anger with every step, but when you're more love than attachment to ego, love is what goes forth from the presence of what you are in droves and waves, changing the world without having to do anything the world notices.

This book can help deliver you to levels of consciousness where you calibrate as love and even unconditional love by simply finishing the work earnestly and honestly, but it only poses the choice for a particular pathway which you must choose to walk down and complete. This book can help deliver you transcendence over the ego and fear in all of its forms, but the choice to walk the road of surrender, forgiveness and gratitude is up to you. What some of you reading this will one day know, is that you're not what you thought you were, and you're not in control of anything, but you're actually that which witnesses and observes everything arising spontaneously in and around your locality of consciousness. Knowingness is different from understanding, just like enlightenment is different from life before the condition sets in.

Jesus was not on this earth to only be a pathway to heaven once your physical life is over. Jesus was on this earth to show how someone can experience heaven while still in the physical body, seen specifically through the quote "the kingdom of God is within." The example of Jesus's life is what this book is all about, and by working these steps and surrendering, forgiving and practicing gratitude, you too will know that Love was not only a person but also with God from the very beginning, just as God is not over there waiting to judge you, but right here and now waiting to show you the reality of Truth found at the end of a totally surrendered life.

The greatest gift that Jesus gave the world was the example for living which delivers a person face-to-face with their creator here and now, and through this book I do my best to take Jesus's message, my experiential life, and the wisdom of other enlightened beings, all to provide an example of how to reach God experientially, and also to provide hope for all reading this, that if what I once was can be what is present now, so too can your life be forever changed by knowing that God is, and not just hoping there's more to life than what meets the eye.

I mention the information about Jesus not to persuade someone to choose a particular religion, but as a means of saying, when you find God for yourself, you'll know who Jesus was and is, and it won't have anything to do with the religion created by man in his name. To find God innately in your life you can't rely on religion to take you there, you have to go past religion and chase after the truth that religion is born out of. Religion is a paradigm of truth. Depending on your religion it may do a better or worse job of pointing towards higher truths, but just like this book, religion won't bring you in constant contact with God, but at best can be something which helps the practitioner move closer to Truth during this lifetime. By practicing a religion or completing this book you're not guaranteed a knowingness of God, for that depends on your karma this time around and other factors with regards to your devotion to finding Truth, but without aids like this book and religion, it's extremely hard to ever know what choices to make next which will lead you into a situation where God stands pronounced on the other end.

This book is a pathway designed to jumpstart your spiritual life and create a working intent leading towards knowing God and not just reading about divinity. If you work these steps integrously, from start to finish, you will have a spiritual experience and awakening which will propel you towards higher and higher truths. The secret of this book and all 12-step groups is that the program found here and elsewhere is designed to have you walking in the footsteps of love, so that you stop just thinking about what you should do and become what you have the potential to be.

My story was not one where I found God through a religion, even though I not only grew up very religious but chose religion as my major in college. Once God was realized internally as all there is, the variable truths within the religion I grew up with re-presented themselves with glaring new degrees of truth and recognizable realities of fact with regards to the Christ and his reasons for coming into existence. But the religion was not the pathway for me to find truth and a real experience with the divine as that which is all there is. Have no fear if you live without the practice of formal religion, for you don't need it to find God, and in many cases, it serves as a block to finding Truth. Just know that at the end of the road, if enlightenment is your chosen path in this lifetime, God witnessed as Love will be what you find waiting for you as the ultimate truth of life.

Just before the final doorway presented itself to what the world sees as Mason, the truth of "I, in greater or lesser degrees of intensity" arose within consciousness, and in your pursuit for finding God for yourself keep in mind one thing, God is only found through love, and being love is only possible through surrender, forgiveness and gratitude. You will not find God within grudges, resentments, wantingness, cravingness, desiring, or any other manifestation of the ego or through attachments to the world. God is not experienceable through the lesser localities of life, for to find God you have to be willing to walk the straight and narrow, make choices which are always based in love, forgive the world and everyone in it, and in the process surrender over all attachments and aversions to life. God isn't a prize you win by beating someone or something. Experiencing God as your reality is a race you have to surrender over winning in order to reach the finish line. God is not found in a "sackcloth and ashes" existence, but in a surrendered one.

We are much more than meets the eye, much more than the ego/mind has any idea about, and yet when we find out the truth about life from the vantage point of enlightenment, one main truth that presents itself is that there's no longer a person who becomes enlightened, but a reality that presents itself without attachment to any belief whatsoever, and that shows you for the first time that what you are is not what you thought yourself to be, with all that's left being a persona within the world but not someone individually operating separately any longer.

There is nothing in this world greater or more valuable than knowing that you are in fact God, and I stress knowing this and not just understanding what's written here. Every "ah-ha" moment in your life are glimpses of higher truths which serve to recontextualize your journey towards the highest truths, but when you know innately that the kingdom of God is within you, you have found the prize that all the money in the world cannot hope to buy. This book is a pathway to God, this book is a roadmap for living a spiritual life, and this book is nothing more than something you can use to help you on your journey towards Self-discovery.

If you have made it this far in the text, then you know what comes next is a worthwhile aspect of each step and chapter:

TRUTHS:

(The Maha-Parinibbana Sutra) *Those who are wise take care of those who are virtuous and faithful.*

(The Upanishads) *The wise person keeps silent and controls his mind. That which he knows, he keeps to himself.*

(The Tao Te Ching) *One who knows should remain silent.*

(The Gospel of Thomas) *Be as wise as serpents and as innocent as doves.*

CONTEMPLATING ON TRUTH:

A particular truth about wisdom is that the wise, through experience, know what to do with next steps more than the unwise know what to do with their first step. The wise have lived many lifetimes up until this point, where wisdom was not gained through guessing what's right and wrong about a choice or an action step, for they have become wise by making decisions over millennia that create a context for now choosing that which sustains and promulgates life, truth. If one knows their self to be a person seeking wisdom apart from promoting such, they are already on the path to further wisdom, but the person who thinks they are the only path to wisdom will find themselves without the knowledge that the steps they take are less than prosperous. In my experience, as wisdom grows so does the knowledge that one's actions at best serve others and the world around them, and although I'd like to say I was born able to help my fellow man and the world around me from day one, the truth is, regardless of why someone incarnates into physicality this time around, and no matter the level of consciousness they come into this life with, helping others who are virtuous and faithful is not a lesson learned until you yourself are virtuous and faithful and have been aided in that pursuit.

In my life, as an example, through a particular work situation this applied greatly, as the employer who paid for my services was not wise as for how to support virtue and faithfulness, and instead chose to stagnate potential through fear of overshadowing their own efforts within the field we occupied, with the outcome being less than thriving for the company. Virtue and faith in another, and guarding such things, does not mean that a person has to agree with the faith or the virtue of that person, nor fully understand their position towards life, but what it means is that when wisdom is present in an individual, they recognize faith and virtue in another are godly characteristics worth celebrating and protecting from the world, not characteristics of humanness worth envying or shining a false light on.

When we take care of those who are wise and faithful, we are taking care of our own virtue and faith. When we feed a virtuous person who needs a meal, we're feeding our spirit and that of humanity's as well. When we look after the needs of the faithful, we're not taking away from the world but giving the best of the world to the rest of the world in more abundance. If you hope to become wise in your choices, first find others who are virtuous and faithful and help them find more truth in their own life. Help them find more peace in their life. Help them find more joy in their efforts. Help them have an easier time with worldly endeavors. Faith and virtue are treasures worth taking care of, treasures worth leaning into, and characteristics worth choosing if one desires wisdom.

Throughout the journey of this lifetime, there were

many instances where I chose to share with another or with the world as a whole the insights I was having and the truth that was becoming clear on a moment-to-moment basis. I would share these insights for the betterment of mankind and for the betterment of my soul, but that story of sharing to help others was only something I told myself so I would have an opportunity to humble-brag about how life was operating for me at the time. There is the story of old that says not to throw your pearls unto swine, but this is not what this truth is alluding to. No, in this quote, the truth is saying what we are is what we are at the time, and what we are at the time is enough.

Not everyone is called to be a teacher or to have the authority of such, because not everyone is here this time around to take on the responsibility of such a duty. We are not to share our mind in the many ways the world now shares it because what most have to say isn't worth a teaching moment, because most, if not almost all of mankind, is unaware that what comes from the mind isn't worth sharing to begin with. In the world of anonymous meetings, they ask that you do not let the outside world know you are a part of the group, and not because what is happening within their meetings isn't helping people. But what happens when someone within the group has a relapse after sharing with the world the mysteries of the rooms which have helped them grow over time? If a relapse happens it's because relapses happen, but if someone proselytizes about anonymous programs far and wide and relapses after sharing with the world the miracle of the 12 steps, then the world judges the 12 steps and anonymous meetings as a whole.

The reason why the wise person chooses to keep to him/herself that which he/she knows, is not because what he/she knows won't help the world, but through knowingness and the ushering in of higher degrees of knowingness, the wise person realizes that the best way to help the world is not to blabber about within it, but to continue on the path towards enlightenment so that he/she can be like the rising tide which helps all ships to float higher.

The best way to change the world is to change what you are, unless what you are is in a place of authority through righteous teaching, and even then, you're not sharing with the world your truth, you're sharing with the world the truth that comes through you at the particular time when sharing is what's called for, and even then, the pursuit of higher truths is never ending. Our thoughts mean nothing. Our minds are not worth sharing as gospel. Whatever comes from the mind is limited to a paradigm of understanding that is best served over a lunch for one, not via a platform that serves the appetites of many.

Knowing is the gift. Knowing is the best place to find one's Self. Knowing is one of the reasons why this life exists. Knowing is the way to more truth. Knowing is how we grow closer to Love. Knowing creates more knowingness. Knowingness is action through in-action. What is knowing? What is knowingness? Why should one remain silent who knows?

For centuries, wisdom like what is shared in this book has been lost on many because the level of truth that abides in the quotes above is often times and almost all the time, not relevant to understanding what the truth within even means, and mostly because the level of truth contained within the quote is unknowable to almost everyone on earth who reads the quote. To know means to have an inner connection to the divine that's realized. Knowingness is a quality of consciousness that operates outside of the mind but within the knowable awareness of the witnesser and observer. The reason one should remain silent who knows, is because to even speak about God as being the ultimate reality of Self, is already set up to fall on deaf ears and leave inquiring souls wanting more from those who speak truth through wisdom.

Once someone who knows decides to speak about what's known, what was once known becomes part of the known experientially out in the ether where neither knowingness nor witnessing reside, and no longer does it remain unchanged through inner awareness within the host where it generated. Meaning, to know something out loud is to share partial truths about the absolute. If someone remains silent in their knowingness, they remain fixed on the angle within which shows them the way to God as known and not just understood. When someone speaks publicly about the way to God or the nature of God, or the truth of God being the "I," the audience is already left wanting more than they came for, because the knowingness of the teacher, regardless of the level of knowingness by the teacher, only provides context and a level of truth to be present, and it's not the words which provide such but the presence of such that provides much. Spoken knowingness leaves more wantingness than it creates completion. To know is the gift. Knowingness for the singular flows forth from beyond as the gift of pursuing what's unknown to many. The teacher has the responsibility to share what's unknown to many, not because there is a different truth present than those who remain silent, but because it's part of their karmic purpose for existing as a locality of consciousness this time around. They're here to leave the serenity of the quiet spaces of knowing and enter into the noise of the content machine so others can find quiet knowingness as well.

Sometimes in life, one has to be aware of what is happening around them as much as what is happening within them. The world as most see it is actually not what they see, but a projection of what the ego presents as a viable way of perceiving the world and all of its goings on. You see, depending on one's current level of consciousness, the experiencer, witnesser or observer sees something different from their locality of consciousness. Throughout the full range of consciousness knowable and realizable on this planet while attached to this body, we only see out in the world what we perceive exists, not what in fact is there. What we see out in the world is a reflection of what we see when we look inside the perceptions, but often, very few take the time to realize this truth, and thus, we have a world full of people who look outside of themselves for something to fix as opposed to within their being for something to realize.

I spent years looking out at the world with the belief that for importance, self-importance, I had to fix something because it appeared broken. Whether I saw an injustice or perceived a slight against a person or group of people, I was searching for ways to save the planet as opposed to ways to know thyself. Gandhi's famous quote, "Be the change you wish to see in the world," is a prime example of the truth relayed here in this thought through another's wording. "The world you see doesn't exist" is another famous quote by Ramana Maharshi, a 20th century sage, which sums up this thought nicely. All the time someone spends looking out at the world as broken or in need of help, is all of the time that the same person could be looking within to provide grace and help for their self.

At a certain point of consciousness, one no longer looks out at the world with anger or a desire to change anything, but they see the world as perfect for the process of undoing karma and making good on the need to grow closer to Truth. The world is perfect for the needs of man's evolution towards the realization of what they truly are, and regardless of a leader in power, the way the wind is blowing, the heat of the planet, or the confines one finds themselves in materially, the world is the exact perfect place for this incarnation of what the world would see as you.

Jesus is quoted as saying, "The kingdom of God is within," and what we as humans often times fail to realize is that Jesus is correct. As we surrender over our wants and desires, attachments and aversions, likes and dislikes, and as we do this continually, the kingdom of God is realized as being within you more and more.

STEP TWELVE

-

Having transcended fear and gained the knowledge needed to surrender over all attachments to the ego in all of its forms, I will be the change I wish to see in the world and likewise am willing to sponsor another in going through these steps whenever the opportunity arises.

STEP TWELVE PRAYER

-

My Creator, perfect is your nature. For everything great and small are displays of your wisdom, your love, and your power. May your will be my own, now and forever more. Thank you for the many blessings of life, the blessing of choice, and for the food provided to me this day. Please forgive me of my sins and provide me the grace to forgive those who've sinned against me. Lead me to recognize you in all I see, keep me focused on you above all else, and help me to love my fellow man without positionality. I surrender all that I am, all I believe myself to be, and all the world says I should be. I love you more and more each day – thank you for loving me more than that.

PERSONAL EXPERIENCES: Joe

It is so easy to get stuck in a world of darkness, where it seems like there is no hope and nobody cares. Like you are a man on your own island. I am here as witness to the truth that God is always with you. You just need to look. Seek and you shall find. Knock and the door will be opened. Ask and you will be answered.

It was not long ago, after losing my dad, I was sitting in my kitchen with tears streaming down my face. I was feeling desperate, helpless and hopeless. It was one of the few times in my life that I prayed in a heartfelt manner to God. I yelled out "if this is all you have for me and what you want for me, I accept. If not, please give me a sign. Your will be done."

Not long after that prayer, Mason came into my life. I knew instantly that there was something different about him. Like an experienced Sherpa, he showed me how to climb out of the dark valley and into the light of the mountain side. As a result of this experience, the guidebook *If You live It* was written.

Like the title states, one needs to 'live it' through thoughts, words and actions based on loving intention. This journey is likened to climbing a mountain. Sure, there will be set backs and step backs. When this happens, don't look at how far you fell, rather look at how far you have already climbed.

I still have some climbing to do, but the view keeps getting better and better. I am no longer a slave to the ego. I am learning to surrender to the will of God and trust Him completely. I have seen too many miracles on this road not to. Like something my dad used to say, "you can't be half in the boat and half out". Lean in totally to God and watch what manifests in your life.

As a word of caution, this road is not for everyone. Many a traveler has been tripped up by Step 4. My hope for you is that you do the work and keep pushing forward. It is not easy. If it was, there would be many more travelers at the top of the mountain and this world would be a much better place. Press on. Choose love over fear. Choose God.

PERSONAL EXPERIENCES: Shy

What life was like for me before finding the steps:

My life was hectic. It was heavy. Life felt like a huge weight on my chest every day. There was a constant internal battle of self-loathing, self-doubt, and a feeling of hopelessness I carried with me every day. That anchor sat on my chest when I got out of bed in the morning, when I looked at myself in the mirror, it was there when I greeted my employee in the morning, came with me in every patient evaluation, my billing meetings, my interactions with making new friends in a new city—it was tethered to me in all of my romantic pursuits. The negative juice from my ego had grown over the years, lending me to unhealthy relationships and tolerating behavior I do not align with. I could never get away from its (my ego) vile suggestions that I was weird and crazy, fat, ugly and not good enough.

And it's silly. You know? I am a bright, shining human being. I'm a physician. My body is healthy, I've got a cool sense of style, fun hair, a killer smile…not to mention, I love living. I'm not some depressed, suicidal addict, strung-out or anything—why was my ego weighing me down so much? I had a great childhood, two parent home, super popular in school, a post graduate education, chief resident, an amazing job, beautiful friends & family that love me, many accolades—I was never poor, I was never hungry, I never had any tragic childhood traumas—what was wrong with me?

I knew there was an internal compass of Love I could follow, but I could never find it buried underneath all the self-hate and my pride! My intuition was somewhere, my Love for myself was somewhere, but I had lost touch with both. I took things personally and I assumed I was the center of every situation, whether positive or negative...and I obsessed over it. My mind was busy and the busyness was exhausting. I had bits and pieces of spiritual texts and quotes I would look at from time to time to quell my anxieties and the hectic-ness, but never an awareness that it's okay to embrace the uncomfortable feelings. I could never get a reprieve from feeling so bad about myself, and it never made sense...why did I feel so bad about myself if I had so much going for me?

Finding a friend in Mason helped guide me through the missteps of my ego, based on his own pursuit of Truth. He helped me see that, despite my seemingly perfect resume and upbringing—my ego was out of control. What I didn't realize is, while I considered myself humble, a giver, and generous--the truth is, my ego was unmanageable. I had a burning desire for everyone's approval, I wanted to be liked, appreciated, and loved. When I didn't get those things, I fell apart. I literally have had breakdowns where I have to detach from the real world and society to heal from a childish romantic relationship not going my way. I am a passionate person and I find depth in anything I can. I took everything deeply personal, because I made the assumption everything was about me. Envy, pride, and an overarching belief I deserve more than others created unrealistic expectations that set me up for a life controlled by my ego.

So yeah, life for me before the steps was heavy and it felt overwhelming, hard, and like I never really belonged... anywhere.

My experience with the steps:

I immediately felt drawn to Deliberate Devotion and started there, finding comfort in the brevity of quotations and simplicity of descriptions to work through the lower energy levels to transcend fear, guilt, apathy, shame. Those are the things that really weighed my being down. As I started to work through the Deliberate Devotion, I found solace in the words that I could re-read over during the day for affirmation that I was "heard" and I wasn't alone in my feelings.

Working the steps was much the same. I finally felt some kind of security, a cradle that I could come to daily in an organized approach, and rest my worries. I could rest the weight of all the insecurities, the constant chatter of my ego—and come to understand that maybe I'm not so messed up, weird, crazy…maybe I'm just a human being with a desire for something more.

There's a method about the steps, and the fact that there is an equation is soothing to me in a way. I have to acknowledge my faults, I honestly admit them to myself and someone else, and then I correct what I can of the wrongs of my past…and move forward. MOVE FORWARD. The idea I could move on past these things was helpful in keeping me encouraged to continue through all the tough parts of working the steps!

With Step 4, I started to lighten the weight on my chest in evaluating past resentments in relationships just by writing them down. There is wisdom and power in writing things down, getting them off your chest. And the moment the words were finally on paper, I deeply began to understand the importance & power of Surrender and Forgiveness. Steps 4 and 5, you have to really surrender everything and lay it all out there. You trust your Sponsor, forgive others of course, but the hardest part can be forgiving yourself. That's been such an amazing part of the steps, forgiving myself and using the concept of "daily/living amends" for the things that arise in the present that need to be addressed quickly.

The steps are well organized and having the author as my sponsor was helpful. I found myself resonating with so many of the thoughts and beliefs, and objectively evaluating my emotions/doubts/self-loathing took even more weight off of me. After step 5, I realized the importance of Gratitude. Gratitude every morning, with Mason's direction was as simple as "Thank you God for my warm, clean sheets, my view of Camelback Mountain, the sunshine on my face, as my dog wags his tail the same way every day. Thank you for this joyful moment." All of a sudden, I was grateful for everyone and everything around me, and when something I perceived as bad happened--though my normal response still occurred to stress/obsess--I was able to sit with the feelings and comfort myself with a mantra of "surrender, forgiveness, gratitude." Suddenly none of the storms lasted as long or seemed as brutal, the veil of the world as I perceived it was lifted--so I could have a taste of how there is so much more to life than what everyone sees on the outside.

People around me noticed the change, the "lightness" I felt was apparent in how I treated my patients, staff, friends, and interacted with difficult situations in my personal relationships.

My life after working the steps:

My life is sweeter and lighter.

I sleep well at night knowing my actions align with my intentions, rather than steeped with fear, doubts, insecurities. And if my actions are not in alignment with my intention or I have wronged someone, I do the work for a living/daily amends and try to right the wrong as soon as possible.

My life has more meaning because I've put more work into it. It's not easy to step back and look at all the things you hide from yourself. This book is work, the work can feel "heavy" but if you do it--the outcome is life changing…so life changing that things that once felt heavy, are no longer heavy. To build any muscle, it takes work I guess. Nothing feels heavy like it did before!

Surprisingly, my life feels less hectic, though I have more responsibilities and things going on. My business and social life are 3 times as busy as when I started the program, but somehow my life feels "easier." Easier in that, through surrender, I am able to remove some of the weight of my self-doubt and place them all onto God and ask Him to take those from me. I can forgive myself for the days I get angry or feel pride, for the times I say or do the "wrong thing" because ultimately it's not about me anymore.

My life is filled with gratitude for where I live, for the small wins in my business, for my beautiful dog that lights up my days. I surrender the worries I have about what if I have to move, what if the business fails, what if my dog dies—and I try to remember the importance of everything in the present moment. You see, in the book there are so many quotes/references to spiritual texts that remind us that the Way, the internal compass of the Self, is always there—as well as God's grace and protection. So I stick with holding onto the gratitude for what I have right now, and feeling sure that God's plan is greater than any plan I could scribe out in my small mind. Every crash of a wave brings in another and things are perfect the way they are, I understand that now.

At times a fear may pop into my awareness and pull me out of the present. The emotions around the fear are still a little uncomfortable, but I've learned from Mason that the fear isn't real…it's an illusion, and it is safe to walk straight ahead. And I do. I keep telling myself "surrender this fear" and I keep doing it. I keep doing it and when it comes back—I do it again. And after I do, I am grateful. One perfect moment leads to the next, and clouds are a pause between sunshine nowadays.

How do I know the steps are working?

There are subtle reminders in my every day that the steps are working for me in how I feel about myself and my relationship to the world. There are overt reminders that the steps are working for me in the fact that my business started to thrive despite being in a global pandemic, my family and friends embrace me and all my flaws with love, I landed a beautiful home during a housing crisis, and I am great at building a social and professional network with my personal flair and ringing true to my personal moral compass.

My 2 cents:

Having Mason's books is like a security blanket. I prefer their comforting weight to all the chatter of ego that kept me anchored down before. What Mason has done is really special, it's like you pick up the text and it resonates with you. As it turns out, the tragic lives and experiences we feel we have, aren't actually that unique—there are only so many permutations and combinations the ego can come up with. So none of us are all that "special" and it's okay to be vulnerable, because that's how we grow. There's a wisdom to the books that provides a base layer, like a primer, that everyone can relate to even if our experiences aren't exactly the same. I never realized spirituality was so scientific until these books came out!

216

Mason is someone who has inspired me for many years. I've always looked up to him, including when he was not sober. 15 years ago I had no idea he was an alcoholic--all I knew is he has something deeply special about him. We don't have any mutual friends, but I'm confident most people probably feel that way around him. I don't know what to call it-- charm or charisma? A gift? For me- it's a feeling of being drawn to someone who is light and Love.

I think that's because he is a genuine and honest person, and he oozes wanting to be better--even when he tells you he calibrated under 200. I feel he has always been a man of humility and his thirst for knowledge is unmatched in anyone I've ever met. He has the capacity to read high level text and recapitulate in a relatable way. Mason has a diverse background of friends, lived in many places around the world, he's lived a life with a ton of clothing & dope sneakers, gave it away to be with nothing, he has a lot of personal/interpersonal relationship experience, he lives what he teaches, he knows what's going on with politics, and he knows 90's hip hop better than me. Mason is also 6'6". Seriously. That is really tall.

Mason has lived life and is open minded. He is non-judgmental about experiences that I trust and want to learn from him because he's willing to be vulnerable. I am sure that anyone who keeps an open mind and reads the two texts will find their heart feeling reprieve from the chatter that weighs us all down. Thank God he chose sobriety, so he can bring this message to people of all walks of life.

The timing in life and the steps, along with Mason's guidance, feels like it's all part of the plan for me to move forward in life. The book will likely feel "meant for you" too— it wouldn't be in your hands if it wasn't meant for you after all.

If You Live It doesn't require an expensive course or a monthly subscription to an app--just your time, the books, a willingness to be 100% honest with yourself & sponsor, and a place to write things down if you want. I learned the concept of "setting an intention" and that has changed my mental dialogue with all my decisions. I try my best to set my intention on something positive and leave the rest to God. Life is so much easier now.

If you're willing to put in the work, even a little work--I guarantee your life will change.

"On this path effort never goes to waste, and there is no failure. Even a little effort toward spiritual awareness will protect you from the greatest fear." -The Bhagavad Gita

REFERENCES: THE STEPS AND PRAYERS

STEP ONE*:* I admit I am powerless over my ego, and my life up until this point has been managed and run by it, but I am ready to find truth despite not knowing it personally yet.

Prayer: I surrender over my ego to Thee oh Lord, in its entirety, and all attachments I have to the belief that I am my mind. Thank you for how this decision will impact my life positively from this point forward.

STEP TWO*:* I have come to believe that a power greater than myself can remove the blocks to transcending my ego, and in and of myself, I do not have the power to do so.

Prayer: I let go of that which binds me, that which I have attachments to, and that which I have set expectations on. Thank you, Lord, for hearing this prayer, and for loving me more than I love myself.

STEP THREE*:* I make the decision here and now, to turn my will and life over to Thee oh Lord. I choose love in the face of fear, your power instead of the forces of the ego, and I accept grace as a gift I don't fully understand.

Prayer: I surrender over this life, my control over it, my desire to control it, the belief I'm in control of it, and my wantingness for life to go the way I want it to go and still reach truth in the end. Truth is surrendered over as I see it in exchange for Truth that can only be experienced, witnessed and observed from your lens.

STEP FOUR: I choose to make a fearless and searching moral inventory of my life, leaving out nothing of consequence.

Prayer: Please help me to see what needs to be seen in order to surrender over what needs to be surrendered. Thank you for the gift of truth, and for the gift of faith in a power greater than myself restoring me to a life transcendent over the ego.

STEP FIVE: I admitted to God, myself, and to another human being, the exact nature of my findings.

Prayer: Thank you Lord for the gift of honesty, the gifts of love, and for the opportunity today to share with you and someone else in the blessings of truth.

STEP SIX: I am entirely ready to have God remove my attachments to the baggage of life found through steps 4 and 5.

Prayer: I am ready for your help oh Lord, and for you to take the things that brought shame and destruction into my life away from who I am moving forward.

STEP SEVEN: Lord, please remove from my life the scars of the past, all of my attachments to what I once believed myself to be, allow me to see you more clearly moving forward, and provide me the grace to forgive myself, you, and the world for where I once felt I was wronged.

Prayer: Thank you for the gift of surrender, the blessing of forgiveness, and for the promise of gratitude to come as a way of life. I love you - thank you for loving me more than I love myself.

STEP EIGHT: Made a list of all the people, places and things I harmed along the way and am willing to make an amends to them all.

Prayer: Thank you for showing me what needs to be cleaned up from my past. Please help me have the courage to be willing to make right what needs to be made right. Thank you for the gift of honesty and for the gift of courage. I love you.

STEP NINE: I made direct amends to who I could and where possible, only doing so free of injury to them, myself, and others in our life.

Prayer: I have fear around this step and I have apprehensions about the relief possible from telling another how I wronged them. I surrender over this fear and these apprehensions. Thank you for the chance to clean up my side of the street.

STEP TEN: Endeavor to do both daily, take personal inventory and where I'm wrong, quickly admit it.

Prayer: I surrender over my desires to be right, to be appreciated, wanted, desired, thought highly of, and all desires to be better than another or lord over another.

STEP ELEVEN: Through surrender, forgiveness and gratitude, I continue to improve my conscious contact with Truth, Love, and all other characteristics of my Creator, praying only for God's will to be what guides my life, and for the power to carry out that will once presented.

Prayer: I surrender over my life to thee of Lord, the steps I take, the thoughts that arise, the beats of my heart, the manifestations of the ego and the workings of the mind.

STEP TWELVE: Having transcended fear and gained the knowledge needed to surrender over all attachments to the ego in all of its forms, I will be the change I wish to see in the world and likewise am willing to sponsor another in going through these steps whenever the opportunity arises.

Prayer: My Creator, perfect is your nature. For everything great and small are displays of your wisdom, your love, and your power. May your will be my own, now and forever more. Thank you for the many blessings of life, the blessing of choice, and for the food provided to me this day. Please forgive me of my sins and provide me the grace to forgive those who've sinned against me. Lead me to recognize you in all I see, keep me focused on you above all else, and help me to love my fellow man without positionality. I surrender all that I am, all I believe myself to be, and all the world says I should be. I love you more and more each day – thank you for loving me more than that.

REFERENCES: BASIC LEVELS OF CONSCIOUSNESS as created by Dr. David R. Hawkins

Higher Levels of **Enlightenment**
Enlightenment through **Victorious Peace**
Joy
Love
Reason
Acceptance
Willingness
Neutrality
Courage
Pride
Anger
Desire
Fear
Grief
Apathy
Guilt
Shame

REFERENCES: TRUTHS

STEP ONE

(The Dhammapada) *Seeking within, you will find stillness. Here there is no more fear or attachment - only joy.*

(The Bhagavad Gita) *Those who find the Way are those who have love and forgiveness in their hearts.*

(The Tao Te Ching) *The Way is mighty, yet people prefer smaller paths.*

(The Gospel of John) *I am a beacon of light to those who see me. I am a mirror to those who look for me. I am a door to those who knock on me. I am a Way for you, the traveler.*

STEP TWO

(The Tao Te Ching) *Achieve the state of a new-born child. Clear and purify inner vision.*

(The Gospel of John) *Unless one is born anew, he cannot see the Kingdom of God.*

(The Dhammapada) *With earnest meditation, purity of mind, and compassionate acts of kindness, you will become an island of serenity which even the greatest floods cannot sweep away.*

(The Bhagavad Gita) *See Me in all things. Dwell in Me as I dwell in you.*

STEP THREE

(The Dhammapada) *Seeking within, you will find stillness. Here there is no more fear or attachment - only joy.*

(The Bhagavad Gita) *Those who find the Way are those who have love and forgiveness in their hearts.*

(The Tao Te Ching) *The Way is mighty, yet people prefer smaller paths.*

(The Gospel of John) *I am a beacon of light to those who see me. I am a mirror to those who look for me. I am a door to those who knock on me. I am a Way for you, the traveler.*

STEP FOUR

(The Tao Te Ching) *Achieve the state of a new-born child. Clear and purify inner vision.*

(The Gospel of John) *Unless one is born anew, he cannot see the Kingdom of God.*

(The Dhammapada) *With earnest meditation, purity of mind, and compassionate acts of kindness, you will become an island of serenity which even the greatest floods cannot sweep away.*

(The Bhagavad Gita) *See Me in all things. Dwell in Me as I dwell in you.*

STEP FIVE

(The Gospel of Thomas) *Your salvation comes from being aware of what is already inside of you. If you are unaware, you will remain subject to death.*

(The Lankavatara Sutra) *One achieves self-realization by practicing mental concentration. He will thus come to the state of Noble Wisdom.*

(The Upanishads) *The purpose of things in your life is not for you to love them, but to love the Self in all things.*

(The Tao Te Ching) *He who identifies himself with the world, receives the world. He who sees himself as the world comes to accept it.*

STEP SIX
(Chuang Tzu) *The wise man moves about, not caring about home or possessions. He lives simply. His feet leave no footprints. Thus, the perfect person is one whose vessel is empty.*

(The Gospel of Thomas) *There was a wealthy man who said to himself, "I should fill my storehouses with grain, and then I will be secure." This was his intention, but that very night he died.*

(The Dhammapada) *There are two paths: one is directed towards wealth, the other towards freedom. The monk who understands this renounces world desires.*

(The Bhagavad Gita) *With a heart unattached to the outer world, those who seek Me find joy and happiness.*

STEP SEVEN
(The Chandogya Upanishad) *Things of the world are transitory. If one dies without first having realized the Self, there is no happiness here, or hereafter.*

(The Tao Te Ching) *As fresh as morning breeze, feeling reborn, I wander here and there without a care in the world. Let others chase after wealth. I am content with the gifts provided by Mother Tao.*

(The Gospel of Mark) *Go and sell what you have, and give the money to the poor. Then you will have riches in heaven.*

(The Dhammapada) *If you wish to be free from old age and rebirth, become an island unto yourself, and eliminate all your imperfections.*

STEP EIGHT

(The Dhammapada) *As long as there is even the slightest desire on the part of a man for a woman, the mind is still imprisoned.*

(The Santiparva Mahabharata) *The wise man ceases seeking worldly pleasures. Thus, he reaches the highest goal.*

(The Tao Te Ching) *If our inner eye were to suddenly open, lust and greed would cease to exist.*

(The Book of Thomas the Contender) *Lust keeps humanity in bondage as long as people seek after those things that change and pass away.*

STEP NINE

(The Gospel of Thomas) *Be wise like the fisherman who caught many fish. He kept the biggest fish, and returned the rest to the sea.*

(The Dhammapada) *Studying many scriptures is pointless if one does not practice the wisdom contained within them.*

(The Bhagavad Gita) *I abide in hearts out of compassion, replacing ignorance and darkness with a shining lamp.*

(Chuang Tzu) *Perfect wisdom comes spontaneously to those who seek it.*

STEP TEN

(Chuang Tzu) *A wise man teaches others without using words.*

(The Apocryphon of James) *Seek wisdom earnestly through learning. Practice wisdom by being faithful, loving, and charitable.*

(The Dhammapada) *The body is a fragile thing. It must be protected against evil by the strong walls of wisdom.*

(The Upanishads) *Understanding immortality, those who are wise do not seek for truth among those things which are impermanent.*

STEP ELEVEN

(The Bhagavad Gita) *At the end of many births, the wise person takes refuge in Me - realizing that all things are the Self. Rare and wonderful is the soul that achieves this state of consciousness.*

(The Tao Te Ching) *Wise is the person who has no preferences for one thing over another. He allows his heart to become empty of desires.*

(The Gospel of Matthew) *Who, then, is the faithful and wise servant, whom his master has set over his household to give them their food at the proper time? Blessed is that servant who remains faithful, for the master will set him over all his possessions.*

(The Dhammapada) *Those young in dharma may lose their vigilance, but those who are wise guard it carefully - for they treasure it above all things.*

STEP TWELVE

(The Maha-Parinibbana Sutra) *Those who are wise take care of those who are virtuous and faithful.*

(The Upanishads) *The wise person keeps silent and controls his mind. That which he knows, he keeps to himself.*

(The Tao Te Ching) *One who knows should remain silent.*

(The Gospel of Thomas) *Be as wise as serpents and as innocent as doves.*

REFERENCES: 4th STEP WORKSHEET

I'm Resentful At	The Cause	What Part Os Self Was Hurt Or Threatened?		Where Was I To Blame?
"We went back through our lives. Nothing counted but thorough-ness and honesty"	*(Why I Am Angry)*			
The names of people, institutions or principles with whom I am angry				
		Self Esteem		
		Pride		
		Emotional Security		
		Pocketbook		
		Ambitions		
		Personal Relations		
		Sex Relations		
		Dishonest		
		Selfish		
		Self-Seeking		
		Frightened		
		Inconsiderate		
				The Nature Of Our Wrong Be specific, e.g.: Lied to Mom Cheated on Spouse

FOURTH STEP INVENTORY: RESENTMENTS

Dear Reader,

With special thanks and humble gratitude, I appreciate your purchase of this book. May the truth found within these pages bless your life and bring you closer to truth in the process.

Mark my words, if you decide to actually work this program in earnest, your life will never be the same again, for in fact, you'll have made the greatest choice possible in this lifetime... choosing to walk down a pathway to God and through the illusion of fear along the way.

You are God's greatest gift, and conversely, all you need to know that truth is already inside you.

Many Blessings,
Mason B. Wooldridge

Having found Thyself, what now says the student? To which the teacher replies: go and be the message.

www.ingramcontent.com/pod-product-compliance
Lightning Source LLC
Chambersburg PA
CBHW021027130626
46552CB00005B/1717